What People Are Saying about

C000026404

UNSTOPPABLE Ⱶ
An Apostolic Leadership Culture And Transformation

Leadership is the most important item on God's agenda for the Church in the 21st Century. Bill Bennot is my friend, and a man whose leadership work I have watched with great respect over the past 24 years. His book on Apostolic Leadership is not at all surprising in its quality, but you will find yourself surprised by his unique approach to the development of an apostolic leadership culture. Not only is this a valuable addition to the vital conversation about Leadership - it is a new view on what "apostolic" means. He defines "apostolic leadership culture" as "simply an environment where the beliefs, values and behaviors of heaven, as represented and modeled by apostles and apostolic teams, become characteristic of a community of people who are being activated to bring sustainable change and transformation to their communities and cities. Further, without giving the plot away, Bill's thesis is that "the purpose and goal of apostolic ministry is to successfully reach and establish people, their communities and their cities in Kingdom truth and order", and he sets out to demonstrate this from Scripture and Church History ancient and modern. What I really enjoy about Bill's work is its emphasis on the apostolic focus being: the planting of churches; the equipping of every member to be apostolic; and the raising of a non-parochial generation to transform Church and World with God's Reign. That this will only be done through selfless, servant leaders working in teams, driven by Kingdom values and focused on God's Mission, is the burden of Bill's book. His piece is saturated with a deep and practical awareness of the Love and Goodness of God as the basis of all ministry. His reflection on Genesis 1-2 and the "3-Team" concept therein is masterful. Although his challenge is urgent, his hope for God's preferable future for the Church is what shines through. Get this book! Read it! I loved reading it - you will be challenged, inspired and grateful that you did.

Costa Mitchell
(National Director for Vineyard Churches, South Africa)

As the dawning of a new millennium unveiled the powerful possibilities of apostolic influence and offices restoration to the church, over a decade later many are still asking the simplest and most vital of questions: "What is an apostle?" and "Why should I care?" This book by Dr. Bill Bennot is the most accurate, thorough, and satisfying revelation on the subject of the apostle yet. The wealth of quotes from Bill's years of personal study and research would alone make it worth the read, but the benefits do not stop there. This book carries us beyond the intellectual ideals of apostolic philosophies into personal depths of understanding and application that yield a truly transformational potential to impact society. I have personally found Bill's teaching on "apostolic capacity" as one of the most enlarging ideas of my current season. Bill is a gift to the Body of Christ and his friendship and insights add to the quality of my life and ministry --- I heartily recommend *Unstoppable Kingdom: an apostolic leadership culture and transformation*.

Dan McCollam
(Founder and President of Sounds of the Nations)

Bill Bennot guides us beyond much of the current writings that address the concept of apostolic leadership. This book not only helps us understand the apostolic ministry, it also gives us biblical wisdom on how apostolic ministry should work in the church today. This should be required reading for any leader who is wrestling with how to implement Ephesians 4:11 in the mission of their congregation.

David Whitehead
(Church Planter and Pastor at Grace Church in New York City)

Bill Bennot's book: *Unstoppable Kingdom: an apostolic leadership culture and transformation* is a valuable study for everyone involved in leadership within the greater church setting. Bennot succinctly and artfully presents insights and applications of how leadership happens and what leaders need to do in order to be transformative in their organizations. His starting point of values and tying together how actions and processes emerge is helpful for all leaders who want to create a better future.

Dr Bruce Winston
(Dean of the School of Global Leadership and Entrepreneurship at Regent University)

I highly recommend Dr Bill Bennot's new book as a must read for every major leader worldwide. After over 30 years of successful church planting and leadership development, Dr Bill is a powerful but humble statesman carrying a special love for the worldwide Body of Christ and its successful completion of God's kingdom advancement!

Bob Weiner
(President of Weiner Ministries International)

Leadership matters; and leadership done in the name of Christ and His church matters even more. The early church and the apostles to lead this church demanded the highest moral and ethical values of their leaders as they desired to follow the example if Christ. Dr. Bennot's passionate book helps us not only to understand the Biblical model of apostolic leadership, but the noble and high call of ecclesial leadership. May we all heed the call to lead in holiness!

Dr Corne Bekker

(Associate Professor at the School of Global Leadership and Entrepreneurship at Regent University)

I have known Dr Bill and Connie Bennot for many years and have seen them preach and live out the Apostolic Mandate in the South African context. They are loved and respected by many, across different movements and denominations, as apostolic leaders who reflect the Father heart of God in a real and impactful way. True apostolic leaders hear from God and know how to embrace and apply all of what God is doing and, in the context of relationships, transform society. Bill's understanding and experience in apostolic leadership and its mandate to bring the Kingdom of Heaven into all of life, is instrumental in realigning leaders' priorities and paradigms. I am confident that in applying the invaluable kingdom principles contained in this book, you too will not just enjoy these revelatory thoughts, but be deeply impacted, encouraged and challenged to bring the kingdom of heaven down to earth.

Gilian Davids

(Senior leader for His People Church, Cape Town, South Africa)

Dr. Bill Bennot's book serves both as a trumpet call and as a road map. It's a trumpet call that sends a clear signal that the church has entered a new season; a fact that many respected Church leaders and prophetic voices have established in recent times.

This means that the old systems, mindsets, protocols, procedures, or ways of doing things are no longer relevant in this new season. God is revealing His new wine skin of leadership through this book.

As a road map, it points the direction and destination the church must travel. But, it also reveals where the church is at, and what it needs, to navigate these challenges and opportunities. It's a new way of building leaders and new way relating to other leaders.

I believe Dr. Bill's book is alerting us to the "... times and seasons in the realm of the spirit... and what the church must do..." This is vital because God is bringing the church into unchartered territory.

God has been preparing and speaking the same sound for a long time. But it takes an Apostle to have the courage to step out, and to pioneer a new prototype of 'leadership structure'. One that will be able to sustain, contained and release God's presence and power to bring cultural transformation. This work shows us the necessary components. It is God's GPS for the hour.

This book has provoked and inspired me. I hope it has the same effect on God's generals or whoever, "...has an ear to hear what the Spirit of God is saying". I am deeply humbled and honored to be asked to endorse this book.

Eugene Ramirez
(Senior Pastor at Victory Tacloban; Philippines)

Not since the time of the early church has the term apostle been more alive and current. It seems that the Holy Spirit is once again restoring to the Body of Christ this vital leadership gift. In this book Bill draws on years of research and study as well as decades of his own apostolic work in South Africa and other nations to provide a comprehensive study of not only the role of the apostle, but the culture that grows up around apostles. This book will help both emerging leaders and seasoned veterans to build teams of men and women capable of bringing about the transformation envisaged when we pray " Your Kingdom come, your will be done on earth as it is in heaven."

Nigel Desmond
(Founder and Lead Minister of God Adventure Church in East London, South Africa)

"Like the sons of Issachar in 1 Chronicles 12, Bill has a powerful understanding of the times and he knows what the church ought to do in this hour. Within the pages of this book, you will gain a clearer understanding of what God is doing in His Church today. Bill will give you practical examples, steps and insights for creating an environment where God's Kingdom can come and His will can be done on Earth, just as it is in Heaven. This book is destined to become a part of the theological foundation for the greatest coming move of God in our lifetime."

Joe Martin
(Founder and Lead Minister of Trinity Church in Dallas, Texas)

Apostolic culture; kingdom leadership; transformational impact: Bill Bennot brings fresh clarity and sharper understanding to these themes that are so crucial to unlocking God's potential in people and organizations. At the same time, his rich experience of three decades at the 'coalface' of Kingdom work in Africa ensures that the message is "fire-tested" and practically relevant. Prepare to be expanded.

Rob Gerhard
(CEO at Umbono Capital)

Bill has devoted his life to an apostolic move of God and to continuous study and personal and corporate development of this lifestyle. Jumping off of a quote which is from this book, that the notion of apostles not operating beyond the first century is a devastating deception, I believe that this book will make a significant contribution to correcting this deception and the fruit of it.

In scholarly and thorough style he leads the reader to the conclusion that the earth is gradually being exposed to believers who have accepted not just an academic understanding of the apostolic but the supernatural mandate which is inherent in it.

Paul Manwaring
(Pastor and Senior Management Team member at Bethel Church, Redding California)

Bill Bennot is a man of passion. He is determined to carry this Redemption story to the hopeless and the forgotten. His insight in leadership comes not from detached observation, but from the dirt and scars of living life in the trenches. He has suffered through adversity and triumphed in grace. He is man for this age with a message of empowerment for God's present and future kingdom.

Jamie George
(Lead Pastor of the "Journey" church in Franklin, Tennessee)

Bill Bennot is a man of sincere hunger for God. His humility to grow and learn is one of his greatest qualities. His book shares the knowledge and experience he has gained along his amazing leadership journey. In his book, Dr. Bennot shares the wisdom on how to advance the kingdom in this generation in strategic ways. It's about the power of God and the power of leadership. I have witnessed firsthand the words on these pages being lived out powerfully and daily through Bill and his leadership in Africa. This book will be an incredible resource tool for all leaders in a wide variety of fields of influence. Be prepared to be challenged.

Bob Perry
(Missionary, Church planter and Founder of the Nashville House of Prayer)

The need for insight and understanding re: 'Apostolic Culture' is critical right now in the body of Christ, and Dr Bill's book takes huge strides in bringing us into fresh light.

Like the Grand Canyon, not far from where Dr Bill once planted a church, this book is majestic and vast in both depth and breadth.

Culture remains critical in reflecting the heart of Christ and affecting real change this book will help many in building the 'Apostolic Culture.'

Roger Pearce

(Lead Minister of His People Church, Johannesburg, South Africa, and African Director for Every Nation Ministries International)

Bill Bennot has always had a huge passion for leadership and leadership development, and this passion is only overshadowed by his compassion for people and his desire to see them discipled into Christ. I met Bill in 1986 at Reinhard Bonnke Fire Conference in Harare Zimbabwe. His desire to impact lives and lead effectively led us into a lifelong friendship. Although separated by distance, we always have a consuming and bonding passion for the common goal of seeing The Kingdom of God come on earth. What Bill shares in the pages of this book are not academic theories; rather they are ideas and ideals forged in the furnace of ministry in the emerging church in Africa.

Tom Deuschle

(Founder and President of Hear the Word Ministries and Lead Pastor for Celebration Church in Harare, Zimbabwe)

Bill Bennot is a respected Leader, father and friend. I have come to deeply regard our friendship and have come to recognize the anointing and leadership qualities he exhibits in his ministry. The experience and fruit upon his life is clearly evident and based on an intimate walk with God. I highly recommend this book to anybody who is interested in extending the Kindgom of God.

Ray McCauley

(Founder and Senior Pastor of Rhema Bible Church South Africa)

Unstoppable Kingdom:
An Apostolic Leadership Culture And Transformation

Published in South Africa by
Faith Story Publishing
3 Flamink Avenue, Mooivallei Park, Potchefstroom, 2531
PO Box 20288, Noordbrug, 2522

ISBN 978-0-620-57293-4

UNSTOPPABLE KINGDOM

An Apostolic Leadership Culture And Transformation

BILL BENNOT

DEDICATION

I dedicate this work to my African home, South Africa. You gave
me a home, a journey and a part of history. Most of what I
have learned, experienced and practiced concerning
good leadership came from among your wonderful
citizens. To the people of South Africa, this
book was written by all of us.
Ubuntu!

ACKNOWLEDGEMENTS

Mom
Thanks for being my hero more times than I can count.

Bob Weiner and Maranatha Ministries
Thanks for modeling the biggest gift of faith I have ever seen. It was my launch pad into destiny.

Ray McCauley
Thanks for making it possible to be in South Africa. Your giving humbled me.

Elders, leaders and members at His People, Johannesburg
Thanks for being my home and family, and for walking with me through so many diverse seasons.

Tom Deuschle
Thanks for being a wonderful friend and modeling unprecedented courage on African soil. I have never walked with a stronger man of God than you.

Paul Daniel
Thanks for giving me the opportunity to be part of history. 'His People' was and is your gift to South Africa.

Regent University
Thanks for investing so much leadership truth into my life, ministry and African home.

Bob Perry
Thanks for the countless days of 'garage worship' that oiled my journey of leadership learning.

Bethel Church, Redding
Thanks for daring to live from heaven to earth, and for loving so many beyond yourselves.

Ben, Adam, Ethan and Melody
Thanks for all your patience and love. Our many South African adventures together are where I grew the most.

Connie
Thanks for being my best friend, and daring to share this life journey with me. You are my greatest earthly treasure, who has inspired me beyond measure.

TABLE OF CONTENTS

FORWORD

There is much in the wind today about 'Community Transformation'. I think everyone is hoping for a revolution or revelation that will bring an ease to the extreme tensions that are pulling so many societal connections apart. Obviously, the answers for earth's conundrums are poised within Heaven's response, yet they continue seemingly unabated. Bill Bennot's book, Unstoppable Kingdom: an apostolic leadership culture and transformation builds toward identifying some of the keys to bring Heaven's resources and effects to the earth through the apostolic governmental structure. While much of his experience comes from leading in South Africa, the model and functions apply in any earthly society. Dr. Bennot crystallizes some keys such as finding an alignment between what's top priority in Heaven and leaders on Earth that will embrace, establish and employ those values and priorities. As human civilization searches for family to be realized and resurrected, it could find the missing foundation of the Church, the apostles. Remove the apostles and you remove the stability of the entire social fabric and structure. Dr. Bennot does a masterful job of pointing us back to the Biblical blueprint of family through a government held together by a loving Father.

Unstoppable Kingdom: an apostolic leadership culture and transformation is a comprehensive look at the development of apostolic leaders and their relevance in today's church and revival movement. Author Bill Bennot does a wonderful job of demystifying a subject many have tried to ignore, or worse, elevated beyond its proper place in the Kingdom. Equally valuable is his ability to identify the things deeply imbedded in every true transformational movement—the goodness of God, relationships, values, family, and generational inheritance. Bill Bennot makes it clear: the apostolic is meant to equip the believer to change the world. Readers will gain insights into their role in bringing the Kingdom of Heaven to their sphere of influence. The church's efforts to improve upon biblical order have failed miserably. This book is a brilliant effort to equip us with the understanding needed to return to Plan A, and complete the commission given to us—to disciple nations.

Danny Silk (Author of *"Culture of Honor"* and Senior Management Team member, at Bethel church in Redding, California)
Bill Johnson (Senior Pastor at Bethel Church in Redding, California)

1

INTRODUCTION

The volumes of books, manuals, teaching tools, seminars, schools and other training materials related to leadership and effective transformation are more than any leader could hope to absorb and utilise in many lifetimes. Why, then, another book on leadership?

As I pondered the writing of this manuscript, I seriously considered that question. My hesitation in writing a book about leadership was further fuelled by the copious amounts of leadership materials already crowding my bookshelves. Meaning, if I could just absorb, practise and impart a portion of what my library offered, any leadership journey would be amply supplied. But thanks to over 30 years of observing, learning and exercising leadership, I understand, at least in part, why more experiences, insights and applications in leadership are welcomed, warranted and even absolutely necessary.

Being a "lifelong continuous learner" characterises the foundry where transformational leaders such as the Apostle Paul, Martin Luther King Jr. and Nelson Mandela were forged. Lifelong learning is required of everyone who longs to see God's Kingdom come "on earth as it is in heaven". This is a journey that navigates through a labyrinth of relationships, responsibilities, motivations, decisions, seasons and changes.

Being a leader and exercising leadership is about having an influence on numerous levels, in many different environments, with a wide diversity of people, in changing and often contradictory conditions. There are just too many variables effecting the application of leadership to justify placing the proverbial ceiling on our learning. Addressing the challenges of leadership in Africa, Gerhard van Rensburg notes that an increase in responsibility and risk has an exponential effect on the complexities of leading. In other words, any new responsibilities and risks that leaders encounter in their careers will require corresponding leadership upgrades. For Connie and me, our transition from doing campus ministry in the United States to planting churches in South Africa required some significant additions to our leadership toolbox. We will be forever grateful for the broad spectrum of leadership input we received while labouring in Maranatha Christian Churches and Campus Ministries. Bob Weiner and the senior leadership of the movement gave us continual access to diverse and complementary leaders.

Just as there are hundreds of ways of combining and applying fats, carbohydrates and proteins to satisfy the human palate, there are hundreds of different combinations and applications for making leading and leadership work.

On the one hand, leadership is like a science: constant, rational and predictable – like mapping out an action plan for a newly developed strategy. On the other hand, its many nuances and permutations make it an art: changing, intuitive and surprising; much like organic leadership, where influence is shaped by compassion, and direction is realised through discovery.

Being a leader can be as basic as an atomic particle or as complex as human DNA. It's a journey full of certainties and mysteries, constants and surprises. It's an adventure like no other. Among the various leadership roles and functions tailor-made by God for stewarding effective and sustainable transformation, we find the apostle and apostolic ministry.

Apostles and apostolic leaders – God's ambassadors for breakthrough and progress – are often misunderstood, underestimated, or even completely ignored. Rather than advocating for the one big leader who harbours a breakthrough anointing, the approach to the ministry of the apostle described in this book focuses on creating a culture conducive to prolific leadership development. It's less about personality and charisma, and more about calling, values, partnerships and environments.

> **Apostles and apostolic leaders, God's ambassadors for breakthrough and progress, are often misunderstood, underestimated, or even completely ignored.**

Therefore, it's about engendering a leadership culture where the measure of success is not lodged in any individual apostle, but in developing and releasing an

4

apostolic people towards effective and sustainable transformation. In his book *The Gift of the Apostle David* Cannistraci highlights this point when he says: "As the needs of a lost world touch the heart of the Father, the Son will gift more and more apostles, who will in turn perfect an apostolic people to reach the world." If Jesus made his first apostles and their ministries foundational for releasing heaven on earth, who are we not to follow this model? Understanding the nature of apostolic leadership is a major step towards creating a transformational environment.

For the early church, apostles were more than just pioneers, miracle workers and church planters. They were social transformers commissioned by God to serve people, shape culture and transform cities. Apostles and apostolic leaders functioned in a sphere of authority that equipped and empowered others. They created environments where a diversity of leadership callings, gifting, skills, personalities and relationships could partner together towards an improved future.

For the early church, apostles were more than just pioneers, miracle workers and church planters. They were social transformers commissioned by God to serve people, shape culture and transform cities.

Not only are apostolic leaders and ministries among God's greatest agents for fostering transformative change, but the 21st-century global context is providing more traction and leverage for that change. The quality of Biblical revelation regarding social transformation and nation-building – which is increasing and being disseminated throughout the Body of Christ – coupled with accelerated access to a global community in crisis, has positioned leaders and believers for unprecedented opportunities.

Among the plethora of leadership roles and functions most necessary during seasons of transformational change are these apostles, apostolic leaders and ministries; and most favourable for stewarding effective transformation is the development of an apostolic leadership culture. *Unstoppable Kingdom: An Apostolic Leadership Culture and Transformation* looks at the calling, focus and impact of apostolic leadership in the 21st century. It draws from Biblical history, Church history, contemporary culture, and over 30 years of personal ministry experience in Africa and the United States.

By combining principles and patterns from Scripture with the ministry experiences and insights of many diverse leaders and believers, this book addresses a category of leadership that is vital for effecting broad-based change. Rather than focusing on specific leadership personalities, traits and abilities, we will look at the most essential values, beliefs, behaviour, actions and processes for creating an environment where people are both transformed and transformational within their communities.

The concepts presented in this book are critical for creating a quintessential Kingdom culture where sustainable transformation can take place. When the Apostle Paul told the Colossians that they were delivered from the domain of darkness and transferred into the Kingdom of God's beloved Son, he was not referring to the celestial afterlife. He was underscoring a present application of divine authority in all walks of life. Jesus said in Matthew 12:28: "If I cast out demons by the Spirit of God, then the kingdom of God has come upon you."

In other words, his Kingdom does not begin with end of the age rewards, but with Spirit-empowered believers encountering God daily, connecting in communities of faith, and engaging a damaged world with transformational truth and power. This transformational environment, or Kingdom culture, can and should be available throughout the Body of Christ.

Donald Miller, in his book *Reinventing American Protestantism*, made an interesting observation: "If Christianity is going to survive, it must continually reinvent itself, adapting its message to the members of each generation, along with their culture and the geographical setting." Although Christianity is much more than a survivor that busies itself by simply shape-shifting to every societal whim, its ability to thrive is predicated upon continuous growth, change, relevance and efficacy.
When the Apostle Paul said: "I become all things to all men that I might win some", he was highlighting the power of the Gospel to relate to and redeem anyone, anywhere and at anytime. History is replete with examples of Christianity's nimble and transformational nature. Howard Snyder describes it as "Christianity's remarkable self-renewing capacity".

From the transformational impact of the early church in the Middle East, Asia and Europe, to the globalising effect of the Protestant Reformation, Christianity has proven itself to be unshakeable in its foundations, strategic in its actions, and adaptive and innovative in its ministries and methods.

As globalisation and advanced technology continue to bring the world closer together, the Biblical mandate to disciple an entire nation is no longer a distant possibility; it is a very real probability. Specific to accomplishing this task are apostles and apostolic teams. Not only are apostolic leaders among God's best ambassadors for transformational change, but South Africa as a nation is poised for this change on a massive scale.

South Africa is a nation of prodigious accomplishments as well as vast, untapped human potential. The purest and most precious treasure of the African heartland is not found in goldmines owned by multinational corporations, but in the hearts of gold owned by no one but God.

Similarly, the real gemstones of the African soil are not the diamonds, but a multitude of men and women who carry in their bosoms the future advancement of Africa. The South African landscape is burgeoning with complex problems, as well as unprecedented opportunities.

Christianity has proven itself to be unshakeable in its foundations, strategic in its actions, and adaptive and innovative in its ministries and methods.

As this millennium progresses, a collective excitement and anxiety hover over the political, economic and social landscapes. From ideological debates surrounding governance to discussions on the growing threats of unemployment, crime and rampant disease, South Africans are searching for answers. If there was ever a time for Christian leaders to be torchbearers towards a hopeful future, it is now.

Costa Mitchell, national director of the Association of Vineyard Churches in South Africa, calls leadership a "watershed issue for the church in this century". Whether motivated by crisis, capacity or opportunity, effective leadership can and must be provided. Any dearth of qualified leaders can be reversed by developing an apostolic leadership culture within a community of believers.

This book addresses those values, behaviours, strategies and structures most conducive to building an apostolic people who will, in turn, cultivate sustainable transformation. The concepts specific to developing an apostolic leadership culture will prove to be applicable and beneficial for effecting transformation in any sphere of civil society.

What qualities are most characteristic of apostolic ministry and the development of an apostolic leadership culture, and how do they play out in a contemporary South African/African context?

For thousands of years, the touchstone was used for validating the authenticity of precious metals. The metal in question would be rubbed against the touchstone (a smooth, black glossy stone). The marks left on the touchstone would be compared with a genuine sample. If the metal was genuine, the mark would be identical in colour and lustre to the sample.

What is the touchstone for the apostolic? Can the authenticity of apostolic leadership be examined, in order to remove any doubts? In spite of the many misapplications of the term, apostles and apostolic leadership have distinctive features and provide irreplaceable benefits to the process of advancing the Kingdom and nation-building.

Among the focuses covered in this book that are most necessary for developing an apostolic culture are: 1) an accurate and applicable understanding of the Kingdom mandate and the apostolic; 2) the essential role of specific values; 3) the relational context; 4) team leadership; 5) global competence and innovative capacity; and 6) Spirit-filled enablement over the long haul.

Although South Africa provides a major backdrop for the ideas and insights presented in this book, none of the key themes are exclusive to the African context. An apostolic leadership culture is not Afro-centric. It is a quintessential Kingdom environment capable of releasing effective transformation anywhere. It is my prayer that this book will assist Kingdom-minded leaders in their quest to see his Kingdom come "on earth as it is in heaven".

At the end of each chapter is a short study section. I've provided questions that will help turn revelation into activation. At the end of the day, it's about turning heavenly reality into earthly actuality.

CHAPTER ONE

The Mandate, Apostles and the Apostolic Leadership Culture

Landing on South African soil in May 1987, with a three-year-old son and a wife in her ninth month of pregnancy, led to a crash course in how the Holy Spirit calls leaders and people to do the impossible. At that time, both Connie and I were novices in doing mission work outside the United States.

Prior to this move, I had only visited South Africa twice, and Connie and I had shared just one mission experience, in Jamaica. We soon discovered that a word from God is loaded with whatever resources are necessary to carry it out. In spite of some real naiveté on our part, the opportunity to engage a new culture in effective and sustainable transformation was waiting for us in South Africa. Until that time, any ability to influence a nation seemed like a distant dream or hopeful cliché. Yet, we soon discovered the favour, authority, anointing and relationships that accompany God's mandate and apostolic calling. We found ourselves joining the ranks of countless men and women, past and present, who dared to believe in and act upon God's call to bring his Kingdom everywhere.

Although Jesus was exceptional, He would not be the exception.

From Jesus' very first invitation, "Follow me and I will make you fishers of men" (Matthew 4:19), until his last command, "Go therefore and make disciples of all the nations" (Matthew 28:19), He taught and demonstrated a way of life that would become a standard for future generations. His words and actions continually emphasised reciprocity and reproduction.

When Jesus said, "Freely you received, freely give" (Matthew 10:8), He was exhorting his followers to demonstrate the same sort of life, ministry and power that they had witnessed with Him. Although Jesus was exceptional, He would not be the exception. Within a relational context lasting some three and a half years, the promises and commands of Jesus became a lifestyle that the disciples were now commanded to take everywhere.

After Jesus' resurrection, He said, "As the Father has sent Me, I also send you" (John 20:21). This holy charge from Jesus to his first disciples, or apostles, is encapsulated in a popular phrase known as The Great Commission. A more contemporary idiom for this commission is the Apostolic Mandate. The term apostolic simply means relating or pertaining to the apostles. Apostles, meaning sent ones, were God's first line of leaders entrusted with furthering the reach of his Kingdom or his Rule.

The word mandate is defined as a command or commission from a higher authority. The mandate from Jesus was to make disciples of nations by advancing his Kingdom everywhere; and his apostles and the manner of their lives and leadership were essential to that end.

The Apostle Paul's position on the role of the apostle reveals both its foundational and perennial nature. He said that God appointed in the Church "first apostles" and that the Church was "built on the foundation" of the apostles. Dr Peter Wagner noted, "The Biblical evidence strongly supports the continuity of the gift of the apostle." (1)

It is my position that apostles create a ministry culture conducive to the development and release of other critical leadership roles and functions, and it is within this environment that God's people become capable of discipling nations. By culture, I mean the values, norms and behaviours that are shared within a community of believers, or as stated by Richard Daft, "a pattern of shared assumptions for how things should be done". By leadership, I mean the exercise of influence that mobilises people towards a better tomorrow. (2)

In The One Thing You Need to Know, Marcus Buckingham defines great leadership as being able to "rally people to a better future". (3) This chapter examines the nature of God's mandate (better future) to his Church, as well as the essential role of apostles and the leadership culture they create.

The Mandate

What is the nature of Jesus' mandate to the Church? Do the current two billion adherents to the Christian religion reflect what Jesus had in mind when He said, "Go therefore and make disciples of all the nations" (Matthew 28: 19)? For some Christians, the mandate may simply mean global evangelism and mass conversions before the return of Christ, where evangelistic lifestyles, strategies and tools become the lion's share of missionary efforts. An example is the 40-year history of Christ for All Nations and Reinhard Bonnke, where over 52 million decisions for Christ have been recorded since the beginning of the new millennium.

For others, it means the transformation of civil society, according to relevant Biblical principles, patterns and processes, for example the Providence Foundation, an educational organisation training thousands of people in a Biblical worldview for the purpose of spreading liberty, justice and prosperity to the nations. Pastor Ray McCauley, founder and senior pastor of the Rhema Church in Johannesburg, South Africa, who is a long-time supporter of Reinhard Bonnke, as well as a great advocate for Kingdom truth in the civil arena, often describes this difference as a church that is both "evangelistically potent and socially significant".

In the article, "Sandwich or Salvation: Is the Social Gospel Biblical?" Ed Vitagliano describes these different approaches to the mandate as a rift between conservative and liberal evangelicals. He notes that, while conservative evangelicals frequently cite John 3:16, "For God so loved the world, that He gave his only begotten Son …", progressive (liberal) evangelicals embrace the more comprehensive Luke 4:18, "The Spirit of the Lord is upon me ... to preach the gospel to the poor ... to set free those who are oppressed." (4)

An interesting distinction between the terms evangelism and evangelisation helps to highlight this point. For example, Albert James Dager's article entitled, "The World Christian Movement", refers to evangelism as the spreading of the Gospel to bring souls into the Kingdom of God, and evangelisation as the saving of whole nations or people groups spiritually and temporarily through political and social action. The former, according to Dager, is about personal conversion and the "discipling of believers that guard Biblical truths and practices vital to sustaining viable relationships between individual believers and the Lord Jesus Christ". (5) The latter, according to the Lausanne Congress on World Evangelisation, is where good evangelism and socio-political involvement are mutually inclusive.

Article five of the Lausanne Covenant states, "We affirm that evangelism and socio-political involvement are both part of the Christian duty." In support of the Lausanne approach, Dr Billy Graham referred to it as evangelism taking on a new meaning. Is civil and cultural transformation really a new meaning for evangelism or is it just a part of Jesus' original mandate to disciple nations?

There are several ways to answer this question. An expected outcome can be extrapolated by understanding the nature of the sender, the details of the message or the role of the messenger. For example, if I were to ask our church administrator to set up a meeting for our citywide executive team, he would focus on all the necessary details, such as the time, appropriate venue, all attendees, agenda items and resources. He would make sure it meets my expectations and the needs of everyone attending. The administrator understands me, the extensive nature of the request and the requirements of his position.

In similar fashion, our heavenly Father, through the person of Jesus Christ and the power of the Holy Spirit, has mandated his sons and daughters to bring the message of the Kingdom to a fallen world (Matthew 9:35; Matthew 10:7). It's about setting up the King's domain or, as Isaiah the prophet said, "There will be no end to the increase of his government" and "Then they will rebuild the ancient ruins, they will raise up the former devastations; and they will repair the ruined cities" (Isaiah 9:7 & Isaiah 61:4).

In *The Gospel of the Kingdom*, George Ladd calls the Kingdom of God "the realisation of God's perfect reign in all the universe". (6) He describes it as God's future Kingdom reaching back into the present age and attacking Satan's domain. Tasting "of the age to come" (Hebrews 6:5) does not mean the complete departure of evil from contemporary society, but rather God making it possible to experience a new power to "prove what the will of God is" everywhere (Romans 12:2).

Ray McCollum, a personal friend and lead pastor for Celebration Church in Nashville, Tennessee calls it living the "awareness of his thereness" in all of life. The great Bible commentator Matthew Henry went so far as to say that the primary intention of the Matthew 28 mandate was to do our "utmost to make the nations Christian nations". (7) According to 2 Peter 1: 3, God provides everything necessary for the successful application of his Kingdom in all walks of life. Paul told the Colossians that it was the "Father's good pleasure ... to reconcile all things to Himself ... whether things on earth or things in heaven" (Colossians 1:19). Jesus, who "will come to have first place in everything" (Colossians 1:18), is setting up his Kingdom.

Addressing the topic of the Lordship of Jesus in his book *Every Nation in Our Generation*, Dr Rice Broocks notes, "To call Jesus Lord means that He is the highest authority in the universe ... He is the King over every earthly king ... his rule extends to every area of life." (8) If he is correct that the Lordship of Jesus means extending his rule into "every area of life", which, according to George Ladd and Scripture is the essence of bringing the Kingdom, then the mandate given to Christians to disciple nations includes declaring and demonstrating the Kingdom of God or the rule of God in all things pertaining to life.

> **The mandate given to Christians to disciple nations includes declaring and demonstrating the Kingdom of God or the rule of God in all things pertaining to life.**

Dr Broocks' spiritual father and early mentor, Bob Weiner, a prolific apostolic leader who has trained and released thousands of leaders worldwide, said that the nation we are called to bring to Christ is not just made up of the people who live there, but it includes the arts, sciences, education, law, political systems, media and business. (9) This means that the Kingdom has pre-eminence in everything — private and public.

Contrary to the opinions of some, this was part of Jesus' focus during his earthly ministry. Both Matthew (Matthew 4:12–17) and Mark (Mark 1:14–15) noted how Jesus focused on the message and manifestation of his Kingdom once John the Baptist was taken into custody. John came "preparing the way" for Jesus, but Jesus came with the message and demonstration of the Kingdom. As He said, "If I cast out demons by the finger of God, then the Kingdom of God has come upon you" (Luke 11:20).

There are at least five significant characteristics of the Kingdom of God.
Firstly, it is a social reality, rather than an individualistic one. According to Noah Webster (father of the contemporary dictionary), a kingdom is a territory and a people governed by a king. Jesus said that the Kingdom of God is something that is entered (Matthew 7:21), therefore, the Kingdom is bigger than the individual. Jesus did not say, "Take up your pole and follow me." He said, "Take up your cross

13

and follow me." Our individual relationship with God (vertical) is tethered to a horizontal life in community. The apostle John framed this even more starkly when he wrote, "… for the one who does not love his brother, whom he has seen, cannot love God whom he has not seen" (1 John 4:20). Autonomous/self-made man is a myth; every person is a combination of the one and the many. The reason why God said, "It is not good for the man to be alone" (Genesis 2:18) is simply because it is not.

Secondly, it is not just heavenly; it is an earthly and political reality. It touches all spheres of life such as government, business, education, family, arts and science, and entertainment. In *Liberating the Nations,* authors Stephen McDowell and Mark Belials argue that the principles in the Bible were given for all walks of life; that they include divine matters between God and man, as well as social and civil matters. (10) Addressing the enormous impact of William Wilberforce on 18th century England, John Pollock wrote, "Wilberforce believed that England's destiny lay safest in the hands of men of clear Christian principle, and that submission to Christ was a man's most important political, as well as religious decision." (11) His Kingdom is about his presence materialising anywhere. It's about every sphere of life being touched and transformed by the grace and goodness of God.

Thirdly, it is personal and relational, not just organisational and mechanical. It deeply values and relates to the uniqueness of every human being. In Be a Leader for God's Sake, Dr Bruce Winston calls love the "overarching value" of leadership. (12) It is a Kingdom rooted in agape love. Scripture tells us that "each person is fearfully and wonderfully made" and that eternal life is about knowing God. The prolific use of familial language throughout the New Testament supports this relational premise. The apostle Paul used the present tense imperative when He wrote, "You are no longer a slave, but a son; and if a son, then an heir through God" (Galatians 4:7). In Chapter Three we will explore this point more deeply.

Fourthly, it is universal. It is intended for all people and all nations. Meaning, it is never parochial or exclusive. The Greek word for nations is ethnos, which means a race, or a foreign, non-Jewish nation. Contrary to the beliefs of some, the Kingdom of God is vested in the goodness of God, and not of man; a goodness that is for all peoples. Jesus made that clear when He said, "… for He causes his sun to rise on the evil and the good, and sends rain on the righteous and unrighteous" (Matthew 5:45). Seeing through the old lenses of us versus them was forever altered by the Holy Spirit being poured out on "all mankind" (Acts 2:17). Although some individuals and communities have appropriated more of what Jesus purchased at Calvary, the fact remains that it is for everyone, everywhere and all the time.

Fifthly, it is fundamentally spiritual and supernatural. Paul told the Romans that the Kingdom of God is righteousness, peace and joy in the Holy Spirit. Jesus said that the Kingdom that comes on earth is the same one that operates in heaven. In *Doing Business God's Way*, author Dennis Peacocke attributes this to man being made in God's image. Dennis argues that, in spite of the fall, men and women

> **Jesus said that the Kingdom that comes on earth is the same one that operates in heaven.**

are created to have the "same goals, desires and ambitions as God", which are to be realised first on earth before we graduate into the future. (13)

The mandate that Jesus demonstrated, which meant exercising this heavenly Kingdom and authority everywhere, is the nature of God's relationship to his people. Jesus modelled this daily in the way He addressed his disciples. For example, when asked by one of his disciples, "Teach us to pray just as John also taught his disciples" (Luke 11:1), Jesus set an astounding benchmark for the capacity of prayer. He said, "Pray in this way ... your Kingdom come, your will be done, on earth as it is in heaven" (Matthew 6:9-10). In this brief, yet profound directive, Jesus presents the Kingdom, "as it is in heaven", as the pattern and standard for what is accomplished on the earth. Meaning, the sky is the limit, where our ideas, relationships and strategies are augmented from God's heavenly storehouse.

Why would Jesus admonish his disciples for becoming fearful during a life-threatening storm (Luke 8)? Why correct them for an appropriate response to menacing conditions? Because the Kingdom authority He exercised to stop the tempest was available to them as a normal part of their relationship with Him. His word spoken, "Let us go over to the other side of the lake" (Luke 8:22), was backed up by a greater authority than any temporal conditions. This is the essence of the mandate and the nature of bringing the Kingdom everywhere. It is the implementation of God's word in all life's circumstances. As Paul said, "While we look not at the things which are seen, but at the things which are not seen; for the things which are seen are temporal" (2 Corinthians 4:18). In other words, the evidence of the Kingdom is the power of God's word changing temporal conditions to line up with his will.

15

While preparing for our move to South Africa in 1986, my wife and I experienced first-hand the evidence of the Kingdom, or the changing of temporal conditions to line up with his will. At that time, we had to go through a fairly tedious process to obtain a South African work permit. At the last minute, some vital documentation went missing, and the processing of our work permit by the South African immigration authorities had to begin all over again. This was extremely problematic, since Connie was about to go into her ninth month of pregnancy.

We needed that work permit within two weeks, but we were told that it would take another six. If it took that long, our move to South Africa might have had to be postponed for another year. However, when God gives you a mandate to do something, the authority to see it through comes with that word. It was the same when God encouraged his young prophet, Jeremiah, with, "I am watching over My word to perform it." (Jeremiah 1:12). When we received a phone call within ten days that our work permit had come through, it became a testimony to the consulate officials. We were told that they had never seen a work permit issued that quickly before. Even something as small as obtaining a work permit can be influenced by the authority of this Kingdom mandate.

The mandate to bring the King's domain is accompanied by divine authority and influence for all of life; as Paul wrote, "For the kingdom of God does not consist in words but in power." (1 Corinthians 4:20). The word for power is the Greek word dunamis, and it is the corresponding divine enablement for bringing the Kingdom into all walks of life. No wonder Jesus told his disciples to stay in the city until they were "clothed with power from on high" (Luke 24:49). The mandate to declare and demonstrate the Gospel of the Kingdom should come, as Paul said, "in power and in the Holy Spirit" (1 Thessalonians 1:5).

Later, we will look more closely at this dunamis power, when we examine the role of the Holy Spirit as it relates to an apostolic leadership culture. Suffice it to say, the mandate to reach the nations is as backed up today as it was when Mark wrote, "And they went out and preached everywhere, while the Lord worked with them, and confirmed the word by the signs that followed" (Mark 16:20).

The mandate for bringing the Kingdom of God into civil society may not mean a perfect (utopian) society, or the reconstruction of the entire social world according to divinely given principles, considering the fact that Jesus said, "For you always have the poor with you" (Mark 14:7). Yet, from the evidence of Scripture and Church history, it will mean the release of God's redeeming power through his people for the purpose of bringing the rule of Christ into all of life. (14) It does mean a quality of living that can override much of the demoralisation and disintegration of entire societies. As Isaiah said, "They will repair the ruined cities, the desolations of many generations" (Isaiah 61:4). It's what Christian writer and social critic Herbert Schlossberg was referring to when he said, "The 'salt' of people changed by the Gospel must change the world." (15)

Benjamin Franklin, one of the Founding Fathers of the United States, said that the introduction of primitive Christianity into civil affairs would change the face of the world. (16) That change begins and progresses through the behaviour and actions of God's people and his duly appointed leaders. Just as the power of nuclear fission requires a technological form capable of containing and distributing its benefits, the scale and scope of God supplying a transformational mandate necessitates a people suitably prepared.

From Genesis chapter one, where God first delegated the development of our planet to mankind, to Acts chapter 28, where the entire island of Malta was impacted through the ministry of Paul, the Biblical record presents an assortment of leaders and ministries as God's primary collaborators towards change and transformation. Among the cadre of individuals and partnerships advancing heaven's redemptive agenda in the earth are apostles and apostolic leaders.

Apostles and the Apostolic

In his book, The Gift of the Apostle, David Cannistraci describes the notion of apostles not operating beyond the first century as a "devastating deception". (17) According to Cannistraci, the failure to distinguish between the uniqueness of the original 12 and the perennial apostolic function has fuelled controversy and confusion, thereby denying parts of the Body of Christ the benefits of apostolic ministry.

> **David Cannistraci describes the notion of apostles not operating beyond the first century as a "devastating deception.**

This cessationist view, or the position that the gift of the apostle ceased at the completion of the canon of Scripture, has led to "intellectual arguments being erected against the validity of contemporary apostles, despite clear teaching from Scripture". Addressing the role of contemporary apostles, C. Peter Wagner said that some cessationists concede that missionaries could be referred to as apostles because they were sent out, but that this would not constitute the office or gift of an apostle. (18)

The use of the term, apostle, has meant everything from the original 12, who were witnesses of the resurrection, to the first generation of Church Fathers after the 12, i.e. Paul and Barnabas. (19) It has also been applied to pioneers and missionaries who opened up new territories for the spreading of Christianity, such as Saint Patrick in Ireland and Hudson Taylor in China. Although the original 12 apostles stand apart, unique and distinct in origin and authority, the evidence of Scripture and the weight of ministry support the ongoing necessity of apostles and their apostolic ministry.

From his exhortation to the Church in Corinth, "... so that you are not lacking in any gift, awaiting eagerly the revelation of our Lord Jesus Christ" (1 Corinthians 1:7), to his instructions to the believers in Ephesus, "And He gave some as apostles, and some as prophets, and some as evangelists, and some as pastors and teachers, for the equipping of the saints ..." (Ephesians 4:11–12), it appears that Paul expected the continuation of apostles and apostolic ministry. Addressing the characteristics of modern-day apostolic ministries, Dr Broocks argues that the office of the apostle is as indispensable to fulfilling the apostolic mandate to disciple nations as is the office of the pastor, teacher and evangelist. (20) In other words, the function of an apostle in bringing the Church to maturity is no less important than the more widely accepted ministry gifts of pastors and teachers. A Pauline approach to the role of apostles supports this position. For Paul, bringing the Body of Christ to "the unity of the faith ... to the measure of the stature which belongs to the fullness of Christ" (Ephesians 4:13) includes the ministry of the apostle. Gaining a better understanding of what apostles are and what they bring to the leadership equation begins where Jesus did, with his first group of leaders.

Luke recorded how Jesus, after an entire night of prayer, selected his 12 disciples, "whom He also named as apostles" (Luke 6:13). Jesus calling his first team of leaders, apostles, rather than patriarchs, elders, priests or teachers reflects the expansive and transformational nature of both the New Covenant and its early proponents. Rather than choosing something more traditional from Hebrew vernacular, Jesus chose a term, Apostolos, and its Roman application, someone sent with the message, authority and resources of the empire. The first-century Mediterranean cultural context left little room for confusion regarding the extensive nature of an apostle's influence and impact.

Just as the case would be in a communal, high-context African culture, the people of the first century perceived themselves as embedded in other individuals within a given social background, therefore, easily developing self-identity and self-perception through the administration of this comprehensive leadership function. In other words, transformation, or the fundamental and significant change of the individual and their culture, was implicit within the role of the apostle. When a fleet of ships was sent from

Apostolic ministry was a contextualised application of divine presence, authority and power to bring the Kingdom of God into all domains of human civilisation.

Rome to pioneer a new colony in a distant land, the admiral, the fleet and the colony were all called apostles. Everything represented and reflected the sender, Rome, and the Emperor.

The Roman apostle or apostolic mandate consisted of the Romanising of conquered territories. It was the global advance and application of Roman culture. Similarly, Jesus appointed his apostles with a mandate to bring the application and administration of the Kingdom of God everywhere. Put another way, apostolic ministry was a contextualised application of divine presence, authority and power to bring the Kingdom of God into all domains of human civilisation.

Firstly, divine patronage was no longer limited within the social construct of one (Jewish) ethnicity or region, but had extended as a covenant for all people groups. Paul viewed the purpose of his apostleship as follows: "to bring about the obedience of faith among all the Gentiles for his name's sake" (Romans 1:5). Gaining new ground was a ubiquitous feature of an apostolic calling.

Secondly, the Law, God's early provision for restraining sin, was replaced by Grace, God's unmerited love and favour towards man for the removal of sin. Paul, who has been referred to as the "apostle of grace" said, "The ministry which I received from the Lord Jesus, to testify solemnly of the gospel of the grace of God" (Acts 20:24). Paul highlighted the impact of this grace when he said, "By the grace of God I am what I am ... but I laboured even more ... yet not I, but the grace of God with me" (I Corinthians 15:10). Fundamental and lasting change was a hallmark of his life and his apostolic calling.

Cannistraci called this escalating and transformative quality, the apostle's goal of "tangible increase and fruitfulness". (21) He said that productivity helped to certify the authenticity of an apostle's ministry. Paul confirmed this when he told the Corinthians that they were the seal of his apostleship. In Churchquake, Dr Peter Wagner called planting and overseeing churches "an important dimension of apostolic ministry". He said that, although the primary calling of the apostle was to declare and demonstrate the Kingdom of God in all spheres of life, planting local churches and establishing communities of faith were primary to that task.

Author Kevin Conner, in his book, The Church of the New Testament, makes the point that not all apostles listed in the New Testament planted churches; yet, all were involved in establishing people in kingdom faith. (22) Cannistraci's definition of an apostle supports this point. He noted, "An apostle is called and sent by Christ to have spiritual authority, character, gifts and abilities to successfully reach and establish people in Kingdom truth and order." (23) Although breaking into new territory is characteristic of apostolic ministry, it's the type and quality of increase and change that is more indicative of an apostle's influence.
What characteristics are most identifiable and valuable to the role of an apostle and the development of an apostolic leadership culture?

While addressing the topic of apostles and their apostolic ministries, John Eckhardt, pastor and overseer of Crusaders Ministries, said that each gift (apostle, prophet, evangelist, pastor and teacher) was necessary, but that there was no substitute for the uniqueness of the gift of the apostle. (24) Paul's use of the phrase, "God has appointed in the church, first apostles ..." (I Corinthians 12:28), denotes their unique position and place in the Church. Cannistraci calls the apostle, "God's first appointment in the membership of the body". (25) He agrees with Eckhardt that each gift is indispensable, but that the apostle remains the most essential and primary leadership gift and function in the Body of Christ. Matthew Henry, in his unabridged commentary of the New Testament, referred to the apostle as the "chief minister entrusted with all the powers necessary to found a church and make an entire revelation of God's will". (26)

Although not exhaustive, following is a list of qualities vital to both the role and function of apostles and the development of an apostolic leadership culture:

1) Apostles are sent by God as a gift to the Body of Christ. The meaning of the Greek word Apostolos, or to send with a particular purpose, and Paul's instruction to the Ephesians, "He gave some as apostles ... for the equipping of the saints ..." (Ephesians 4:11–12), reflect the divine ordination and validation of an apostle's ministry. In his book, *Sent Out*, Larry Caldwell called God "a sending God", and said that any understanding of apostleship should begin with a sending that is "rooted in the very character of God". (27)

In almost every letter to the various churches, Paul begins by introducing his apostleship as being "by the will of God" (Ephesians 1:1). So significant was this aspect of his ministry that Paul told the Galatians that he was "an apostle (not sent from men nor through the agency of man, but through Jesus Christ and God the Father ...)" (Galatians 1:1). Secondly, the apostle is a gift to the entire Body of Christ and not to just one local church.

The apostle is a gift to the entire Body of Christ and not to just one local church.

Conner noted that apostles cannot be sectarian. He said, "They should have a vision for the whole Body of Christ." (28) Dr Peter Wagner, in *Churches that Pray*, highlighted the need for unity among pastors in a city, who he calls the "spiritual gatekeepers of the city". (29)

The primary call of the apostolic is to bring the Kingdom of God into all the domains of city life; of which planting local churches is only one part, albeit an important one. Rather than serving the parochialism of one individual congregation, apostles reap unity within the broader Body of Christ as they focus on bringing the Kingdom to their city or region. Cannistraci argued, "A true apostle ... wants to spend time growing through association (with) and strengthening the Church through efforts of co-operation and unity." (30)

Paul confirmed this apostolic characteristic when he admonished the Corinthians for their divisiveness. He said, "For I have been informed ... that there are quarrels among you ... each one of you is saying, 'I am of Paul,' and 'I of Apollos,' and 'I of Cephas,' ... Has Christ been divided?" (1 Corinthians 1:11–13). I contend that Paul's words to the Ephesians about apostles, prophets, evangelists, pastors and teachers building up the Body of Christ until it attains to the unity of the faith, was for the Body of Christ at large, and not just for one local congregation. For an apostle, unity is not a goal; it is the fruit of bringing the Kingdom.

2) Apostles and apostolic ministry are relationally grounded. Paul told the Philippians that he longed for them with the affection of Christ Jesus (Philippians 1:8), and that he considered all things as rubbish in comparison to his desire to know Christ (Philippians 3:8). Paul's relational model was reflected in both his ongoing pursuit of Jesus and his familial approach to the Church. If the Kingdom of God is "primarily relational", rather than functional, as argued by Graham Cooke in *The Divine Confrontation*, then the apostolic, the Kingdom's primary proponent, is best realised and applied in the relational context. Bible teacher Dick Iverson called relationships the "basis of all spiritual authority". (31)

> **It is interesting to note that Paul never referred to people as simply 'disciples'. For him, making disciples was a family affair.**

Paul's rhetorical style reflects the centrality of his ongoing intimacy with Jesus and his fatherly role among the churches. It is interesting to note that Paul never referred to people as simply "disciples". For him, making disciples was a family affair. His intentional use of familial language is noteworthy. He reminded the Corinthians, "For in Christ Jesus I became your father" (1 Corinthians 4:15). In Chapter Three, we will examine this relational quality more extensively.

3) Apostolic ministry is catalytic for multiplying new leaders and mobilising the Body of Christ. Whether it was the apostle Paul exhorting Timothy to "entrust these to faithful men who will be able to teach others" (2 Timothy 2:2), or the apostle Peter reminding the believers in Asia to employ their gifts "in serving one another as good stewards of the manifold grace of God" (1 Peter 4:10), the New Testament record shows apostolic ministry focusing on the recognition and release of leaders. This may be one of the most valuable contributions for bringing the Kingdom of God into all spheres of life.

Although rooted in apostolic leadership, apostolic ministry is not confined to a few veteran apostles. The Greek word apostello or being sent is used to describe a much larger group of people. What Cannistraci calls an "apostolic people", Luke describes as "those who had been scattered (and) went about preaching the word" (Acts 8:4). (32) Rather than resting on the laurels of their personal ministry successes, apostles will motivate and equip entire communities towards effective transformation. In *The Rise of Christianity,* Rodney Stark, author and professor of Sociology at the University of Washington, asked the question, "How did a tiny and obscure messianic movement from the edge of the Roman empire dislodge classical paganism and become the dominant faith of Western civilisation?" Stark's research revealed that one of the primary means of growth was through the united and motivated effort of Christians; through a multitude who shared the good news with their friends, relatives and neighbours. He said, "Christianity ultimately survived and continues to prosper, through the power of the personal influence of the people who live according to its principles." (33)

4) The ministry of an apostle is accompanied by the confirming evidence of signs, wonders and miracles. Dr Donald Guthrie, author of The Apostles, referred to the miracles in the book of Acts as the apostles "following in the steps of the Master". (34) He said that it was an important part of the early Church and an integral part of its growth. Paul even defended his apostleship to the Corinthians by stating, "The signs of a true apostle were performed among you with all perseverance, by signs and wonders and miracles" (2 Corinthians 12:12).

In *The New Apostolic Churches,* Dr Peter Wagner makes the argument that apostles and apostolic ministries are on the rise. Highlighting 18 different church-planting movements, he said even the new apostolic churches that do not consider themselves charismatic have a "sincere openness to the ministry of the Holy Spirit". (35) While addressing the issue

> **Apostolic order without apostolic power is to be questioned.**

of apostolic teams, Bill Johnson, senior pastor for the Bethel Church, Redding, CA, warned, "Apostolic order without apostolic power is to be questioned. Order based on Biblical principle that is lacking Biblical power is tragic at best and deceptive at worst." (36) The gospel of the Kingdom, which Paul said does not come "in word only, but also in power and in the Holy Spirit" (1 Thessalonians 1:5), continues to penetrate and impact some of the most difficult places in the world, and signs, wonders and miracles are part of this occurrence. In Chapter Six, this supernatural quality will be examined more closely.

5) Apostles are builders of teams. Dr Jonathan David, founder of the Apostolic Network of Prophetic Churches and Ministries based in Johor, Malaysia, says the

apostle's ability to gather or build a skilful team is one of the most distinctive features of their ministry. (37) Paul's apostolic ministry models this point. From the earliest phase of Paul and Barnabas pioneering new territories (Acts 13), to the developing of churches through the appointment of elders (Acts 14), to the apostles and elders gathering to discuss issues affecting the entire Body of Christ (Acts 15), partnerships between apostles and other leaders were quite prominent. Cannistraci said, "No balanced apostle seeks to isolate himself from others." (38)

After more than 30 years' experience with apostolic ministry in the United States and Africa, I have never seen an apostle in isolation. The very nature of apostolic ministry, which is to declare and demonstrate the Kingdom of God everywhere, requires a love for the Body of Christ, a diversity of leadership personnel and a willingness to cover entire geographical regions.

6) Apostles, although not entirely cross-cultural, are usually regional or global in their ministry scope. Although Peter wasn't cross-cultural in his apostleship like Paul, it was he who was first used by God to sweep away the divide that still existed between Jews and Gentiles. Donald Guthrie, in his commentary on Peter's encounter with Cornelius, a Roman military officer, noted how God used Peter to show that He "makes no distinction among nations —Jews and Gentiles are on the same basis". (39) Guthrie argues that Peter's personal experience with Jesus (one of the original 12), together with the visible demonstration of the Holy Spirit filling the Gentiles, won the day against the nationalist prejudices of the circumcision party. (40)

This cross-cultural/global characteristic of apostolic leadership is reflected in the rise of the Antioch church as a pattern for the future. (41) Dr William S. Bernie asserts that the church in Antioch was the home base for Paul, "the greatest missionary and the greatest evangelist who ever lived". Antioch became the "fountainhead from which most of the churches of the New Testament sprang". (42) One of the qualities most apparent in the Antioch church was the cultural and social diversity of its leadership.

In Acts 13, we find Barnabas, who is a Levite; Simon (who is called Niger), from African descent; Lucius, probably a Gentile from the African colony of Cyrene; Manaen, from a socially privileged background with childhood connections to King Herod; and Saul (Paul), a Pharisee who had lived in a Gentile-dominated culture. This highlights the cross-cultural character of the apostles, as well as the community influenced by their leadership. With the explosion of accessible and affordable high-speed communication and transportation, the apostolic quality of working in diverse cultural environments is vital for reaching and serving the 21st century global village.

Apostles are called by God to be an ever-present feature in bringing the Kingdom of God on earth as it is in heaven. From the meaning of the Greek word Apostolos to the unique qualities and characteristics of an apostle, the evidence strongly suggests that the role of apostolic ministry is irreplaceable. An apostle's calling (from God and to the Body of Christ), coupled with their multicultural ability, will broaden the scope of their influence, while the quality of their relationships and partnerships (leaders and teams) will deepen the extent of the Kingdom's impact.

These distinctive traits, together with what Cannistraci calls "an apostle's unique and dependent relationship with the Holy Spirit", do more than just authenticate and activate the ministry of an individual apostle. (43) They become characteristic of an apostolic people, i.e. the Church. In other words, as Cannistraci states, "The emerging company of apostles and apostolic people will be a world-changing force." (44) The strength of that force stems from the function of an apostle, as well as a church environment harbouring apostolic traits.

The emerging company of apostles and apostolic people will be a world-changing force.

This church or ministry environment where apostolic leadership is being developed and demonstrated is a leadership culture conducive to effective and sustainable transformation. It is what Paul meant when he reminded the Ephesians that the purpose of the apostle, prophet, evangelist, pastor and teacher is to equip the saints for the work of ministry (Ephesians 4:11-12). This leadership culture will be examined in the next section.

Apostolic Leadership Culture

Richard Daft, author of *The Leadership Experience*, defined culture as the "key values, assumptions, understandings and norms" that are shared within a community of people. The culture is the way we are, or, "how we do things around here". (45) Every organisation or community of people has a culture, and that

25

culture determines how people relate to one another internally, as well as how they perceive and engage with their external environment.

When Connie and I first moved to South Africa, the culture of hospitality was amazing and humbling. You could not visit a home without the minimum of tea, coffee and rusks being served. We found out very quickly that it was nothing short of rude to not offer some form of sustenance when visitors arrived. Much of this neighbourly generosity can be attributed to the communalism common to African culture. In spite of the aberrations of apartheid, and the separation and isolation of people, South Africans have this organic quality of showing hospitality to strangers. They tend to take each other much more personally than those from more individualistic societies. These African cultural characteristics continue on as an older generation of leaders models them to the next generation. As Erwin McManus notes, "Our communities reflect our leadership." (46)

In like manner, the presence of apostolic leaders serving in local churches shapes a culture, or a way of living, that reflects Kingdom values and beliefs. Paul called himself "a model" that the Thessalonians would follow (2 Thessalonians 3:9). The writer of Hebrews even commanded the believers to be imitators of the faith of their leaders (Hebrew 13:7). Of course, Paul only expected the Corinthians to follow him as he followed the Lord (I Corinthians 11:1). What does this apostolic leadership culture look like, and how does it develop in a community of believers? Earlier, we defined apostolic as "the characteristics pertaining to an apostle and their ministry". We also looked at the Greek word, apostello, meaning sent, which is applied to a group of people, or a community of believers. As Cannistraci mentioned, "They may not be apostles, but they can be apostolic." (47) He said, "In a unique way, everyone who follows Christ as a disciple is part of the apostolic company." (48) Jesus affirmed the apostolic call for all believers in his prayer to the Father. He said, "As You sent (apostello) Me into the world, I also have sent (apostello) them into the world ... I do not ask on behalf of these alone, but for those also who believe in Me through their word" (John 17:18-20). Jesus was paving the way in prayer for his people to be an apostolic community.

If we define culture as the values, assumptions and norms shared within a community of people, and leadership as the influencers that mobilise people towards a better future, then an apostolic leadership culture is an environment where beliefs, values, behaviours and actions specific to an apostle's calling are characteristic of a community of people who are being mobilised towards positive change and transformation. In *Building People, Building Dreams*, Pastor Tom Deuschle, President of Hear the Word Ministries based in Harare, Zimbabwe, wrote, "Every member of the Body of Christ is responsible for establishing the Kingdom of God." (49) Hear the Word Church in Zimbabwe has become a beacon of transformation in that crisis-torn nation.

From their work among tens of thousands of Mozambican refugees in the 1990s to their current transformational efforts in government, business, finance, education and healthcare, this community of believers is bringing the Kingdom to one of the most devastated nations in Africa. This is the essence of an apostolic leadership culture: that from within a community of believers, an ongoing supply of new leaders with diverse callings, gifting and skills, are encountering relationships, resources and opportunities that empower, equip and enable them to facilitate effective

> **An apostolic leadership culture is an environment where beliefs, values, behaviours and actions specific to an apostle's calling are characteristic of a community of people who are being mobilised towards positive change and transformation.**

transformation within an entire region. Cannistraci argues that God will not just call a handful of apostles to change the world; rather, He will establish a vast company of apostolic people. (50)

As the evidence suggests, apostles are irreplaceable for fulfilling the mandate. Yet, it will require more than just the restoration of individual apostles to see the Kingdom of God come on the earth as it is in heaven. Paul made it clear that "the equipping of the saints for the work of service" was paramount to the Body of Christ gaining "the measure of the stature which belongs to the fullness of Christ" (Ephesians 4:12-13); a stature capable of revealing "the manifold wisdom of God" to the rulers and authorities (Ephesians 3:10).

Howard Snyder said in *The Problem of Wineskins* that the Church as a people will be the verification of the message proclaimed. (51) John Howard Yoder, a Mennonite scholar, described the work of God as "the calling of a people". (52) Paul strongly emphasised the significance of a church's many ministries, gifts and members when he admonished the Corinthians with, "the members of the body which seem to be weaker are necessary" (I Corinthians 12:22).

In *Managing the Non-Profit Organisation*, Peter Drucker hit the proverbial "nail on the head" when he said, "People determine the performance of an organisation. No organisation can do better than the people it has." (53) An apostolic leadership culture is more about everyone a leader and not just a few significant positions and functions.

Although most leaders operate in specific positions and roles, an apostolic leadership culture takes into consideration the influence and impact of every human life. This apostolic ethos was reflected in the Jesuit approach to leadership, which said, "Everyone is a leader." Former Jesuit and author Chris Lowney addressed one of the keys to the global and transformational successes of the Jesuits in *Heroic Leadership* by saying that the Jesuits treated everyone as a "potential leader" with the power to positively influence the world around them. (54) According to the Jesuits, "Leadership springs from within; it's as much about who I am as what I do. Leadership is not an act; it is my life." (55) It's about materialising the divine image resident in every human being. It debunks the "great man" theory of leadership and, instead, fosters an environment where "best qualities" can be brought out of every person.

> **It debunks the 'great man' theory of leadership and, instead, fosters an environment where 'best qualities' can be brought out of every person.**

This is a critical part of the apostolic culture, where every individual can be honoured and offered the opportunity to be a creator of change. According to James O' Toole, honour creates an atmosphere of trust, which improves the overall quality of the individual's contribution, as well as the relationship. (56) Being a leader is not measured by the scale or scope of the opportunity, "but by the quality of the response". (57)

One little-known disciple from Damascus, Ananias, never led a church or marshalled the multitudes, but through one faithful act of obedience, he launched the early Church's greatest apostolic leader, the apostle Paul (Acts 9). This is what leadership consultant Gerhard van Rensburg was referring to when he said that leadership was not founded on the function of a position, but on the "will" to improve the conditions of any situation as a service to others. (58) This belief that every member is a potential leader is at the heart of an apostolic leadership culture, and is developed within a community of believers who share and demonstrate the values, beliefs and norms commensurate with an apostolic ethos.

Dr Peter Wagner sees this community of believers as the primary incubator for the apostolic culture. He called the Bible's position on every member a minister a vital characteristic of the New Apostolic Reformation that emerged at the close of the 20th century. (59) This critical feature gains better traction within a local church environment that fosters Kingdom (apostolic) values, relationships, strategies and actions.

Rather than falling prey to what Cannistraci calls "success seminar burnout", (60) where church leaders and pastors run from one conference to the next, looking for the newest programmes, tools and techniques to gain the coveted prize of increased church membership, growth within an apostolic culture results from a community of believers who:

- are focused on a daily encounter with Christ
- imbibe the value of every human life
- connect into familial relationships within the Church
- view all of life as a stewardship accountable to God
- see leadership as the calling of every member
- live a life dependent on the Holy Spirit
- view their local church as only one part of a bigger Kingdom that is advancing into a city or region.

It is within this environment that apostles combine their gifts with the gifts of others in the Body of Christ to properly establish the Kingdom.

Finally, the apostolic charge of every member a minister presupposes each believer's personal capacity for hosting heaven and bringing the Kingdom. One of the most provocative revelations for catalysing heaven on earth is found within our own design. When Paul told the Ephesians that God was able to do

One of the most provocative revelations for catalysing heaven on earth is found within our own design.

"far more abundantly beyond all" that they could ask or think, according to the power that works within them (Ephesians 3:20), he was referring to the staggering capacity resident in every individual.

Apostolic Capacity

In Mark 5, we read how Jesus and his disciples had travelled through a treacherous storm on the Sea of Galilee. They ended up on the shores of Gadara, and were met by a man who was so severely demonised that no one could restrain him. An intriguing dialogue takes place between Jesus and the unclean spirits (demons) within the man. The story ends with the man being fully delivered from his hellish torment.

At first glance, it seems to be a simple but powerful example of personal deliverance. Yet, a closer look reveals something even more amazing than the displacement of demonic entities. In Mark's narrative, we find a conspicuous amount of references made to quantity or size. For example, when Jesus asked the unclean spirit what its name was, the demon responded, "My name is Legion; for we are many" (Mark 5:9, italics added). A "legion" was a Roman military term used for 6 000 soldiers. In other words, there were thousands of demonic spirits camping out in that one man.

Then Mark describes a nearby herd of swine as being "large" (Mark 5:11). He continues his emphasis on quantity by estimating the size of the herd to be at around "two thousand" pigs (Mark 5:13). When Jesus commanded the demons to leave the man, they immediately entered into the herd. Once the demons had entered the pigs, the entire herd rushed down the steep embankment and was drowned in the sea.

What often goes unnoticed in this story is that it took 2 000 pigs to contain the demons that occupied just one man. What does that suggest about the design and capacity of the human soul and spirit? What does that reveal about how "fearfully and wonderfully made" (Psalm 139:14) each person really is? The heavens may declare God's glory, as the psalmist writes, but every individual has been created to contain it. Here is a truth that the natural mind will battle to comprehend, but it is true nonetheless.

What is unseen in a single human being has as great a capacity for God as the physical universe has for stars. In other words, the physical universe is a mere

UNSTOPPABLE KINGDOM

reflection of each person's vast capacity for who God is. This truth is supported by Kingdom principles, the testimony of Scripture, human physiology and life experiences.

Let's begin with a Kingdom principle that says the "internal is causative to the external". According to this principle, what we see fabricated in our external world is only a creation, or an effect of the internal world of the human soul and spirit. From our forms of government to how we express ourselves in the arts and sciences, the external spheres of human activity and creativity are influenced and shaped from within.

Authors McDowell and Belials describe the origin of all government as beginning in the heart of man. (61) Meaning, how we govern our conscience, will, character, thoughts, ideas, motives, convictions, attitudes and desires shapes our many forms of human government, e.g. family, church and civilian life. The writer of Proverbs 4:23 said, "Watch over your heart with all diligence, for from it flow the springs of life." Everything seen in

> **What is unseen in a single human being has as great a capacity for God as the physical universe has for stars.**

this material universe initially came out of God's nature and character, while everything manufactured since, came out of man.

All our products and technology began as a thought, an idea, which partnered with human initiative, hard work and perseverance. In other words, man's mind and character took the raw material found in creation (that which came out of God) and created something new.

Author and poet Amy Lowell reflects this partnership by defining Art as "the desire in man to express himself, to record the reactions of his personality to the world he lives in". (62) Companies like Microsoft and Apple owe their existence and impact to this internal to external process. The creative energies and innovative capacities of their workforce make their success possible. The iPad was an idea before it was a successful product. The many functions of our human physiology are generated from well below the skin, while our skills and abilities depend on our mental and emotional processes. The vast majority of who we are and what we do gets generated from the inside out, while our copious accomplishments

31

find their origin in the repository of the human soul. The extent of our human capacity is further illustrated by how God approached one Chaldean by the name of Abram.

God's very first recorded conversation with Abram is loaded with the promise of exponential growth and blessing. He said to Abram, "I will make you a great nation ... and in you all the families of the earth will be blessed" (Genesis 12:2-3). Later on in the relationship, God makes a stunning pronouncement. He says to Abraham, "I will greatly multiply your seed as the stars of the heavens" (Genesis 22:17, italics added). In other words, God compares Abraham's future blessing to the number of stars in the universe.

Using the metaphor of the stars, let's consider the enormity of that promise. With the help of the world's most powerful telescopes such as the Hubble Space Telescope or the newer Large Binocular Telescope, some astronomers have estimated the number of stars at 10 to the 25th power. That is 10 million billion, billion stars.

To gain some perspective on the magnitude of that number, let's look at how long it would take to count all the stars. If we could count 20 stars per second, it would take 10 million billion years to count all the stars. The sheer volume associated with all these stars is incomprehensible, and yet God told Abraham that his offspring would be like the stars. Now, we may exaggerate or use hyperbole to make a point, but God is not doing that here. Meaning, the number of stars in the universe represents a corresponding quantity in our relationship to God.

Although God's promise to Abraham included his direct offspring (the nation of Israel), the metaphor used represented something far beyond his natural descendants. Paul told the Galatians that implicit within the promise to Abraham was the justification of the Gentiles through faith. He went on to write, "In Christ Jesus the blessing of Abraham might come to the Gentiles" (Galatians 3:14).

Even though the whole of mankind was included in the promise, the blessing of Abraham cannot be understood as just a number, because the population on the planet is infinitesimal compared to the number of stars. Paul went on to remind the Galatians about the life of sonship. He said that, if we are sons, then we are heirs of God, and not just of Abraham. Meaning, the blessings of Abraham is about the vast magnitude of life that we can experience in relationship to God. The promise to Abraham is a spiritual promise, which is understood and experienced through our spiritual capacity. The amazing capacities of every person are evident on three levels: body, soul and spirit.

If we begin with just one human body, what we discover is astounding. Our physical bodies are much more than just a torso and a few dozen appendages. They consist of millions of parts and trillions of cells harmonising perfectly to do some remarkable things. The mass, strength and speed found within our human anatomy are quite amazing. There are about 60 000 kilometres of capillaries in the human body. If extended end to end, one person's vascular system would navigate around the globe several times. Of course, our nervous system would more than double that. The length of the DNA code from just one individual would cover the distance to the moon about 20 times.

If we begin with just one human body, what we discover is astounding.

When God told Adam and Eve to populate the earth, He was well aware of Adam's reproductive capacities. One man's testicles can produce enough sperm to replicate the earth's current population in just six months. We often hear about how slow and weak mankind is relative to the animal kingdom, but aspects of our human physiology demonstrate amazing speed and strength. Human bone is four times stronger than concrete. A small block of bone, no bigger than a matchbox, can support the weight of nine tons. When we sneeze, we can generate a wind speed of over 160 kilometres per hour.

The remarkable capacity of our physiology is also evident in some amazing human feats. A Chinese martial arts master named Fu Bingli did 12 push-ups using only one index finger. In 1982, in Lawrenceville, Georgia, Angela Cavallo lifted a 1964 Chevrolet Impala off of her son. There are countless examples of people walking on fiery coals or thrusting long swords down their throats, without any apparent injury. Then we have exceptional individuals, called savants, such as Kim Peek, the inspiration behind the film *Rain Man*. He read and remembered 12 000 books. Most astonishing was his ability to read two different pages simultaneously with just one eye on each page. These physical accomplishments are evidence of our body's enormous capacity.

As amazing as the human body is, its output seems small in comparison to our intellect, will and emotions. Meaning, what's found in the soul of man is the difference between swinging in the trees and building skyscrapers; between primitive living and creating civilisations. In many sports requiring great physical prowess, an individual with a stronger mind will often prevail over someone who has the bigger and stronger body.

I'm reminded of one of the greatest sporting feats I have ever seen. Mark Robinson, a close friend, and a South African power-lifting and wrestling champion, was invited to Japan to participate in the World Sumo Wrestling Championships. Although Mark, according to normal standards, was a big, strong man with great athletic ability, his size was diminutive in comparison to the current world champion. Mark was just 1,8 metres tall and weighed around 140 kilograms, while the world champion, Emmanuel Yarborough, was close to 2,1 metres tall and weighed around 317 kilograms. Mark was physically dwarfed by the champion.

Amazingly, Mark made it to the finals against this mammoth of a man. Prior to the final match, while watching others compete against the world champion, he noticed that they would often hesitate. This allowed the champion to get the jump on them, and led to their defeat.

There is more of God in you than there is evil in the world.

Mark decided to strike first. When he slammed into this present-day Goliath, he caught a glimpse of fear in his eyes. From that point on, he dominated this giant and won the world championship. This is a good illustration of how much stronger the soul is than the physical body.

Even the seemingly impossible feat of a mother lifting a car off of her son can be attributed to the power of human emotion and will. What we feel, know and decide has put men on the moon and turned deserts into agricultural paradises. Of course, just when we think the human soul is unmatched in its abilities, we run right into the human spirit, which is infinitely more capacitated.

The apostle John recorded some amazing insights regarding the magnitude of the human spirit. After Jesus said, "From his innermost being will flow rivers of living water" (John 7:38), John wrote, "But this He spoke of the Spirit, whom those who believed in Him were to receive" (John 7:39). In other words, coming out of the spirit of man would be a constant flow of the Holy Spirit.

34

The volume of that stream only becomes apparent when we look at what John wrote in his first epistle. He said, "You are from God, little children, and have overcome them; because greater is He who is in you than he who is in the world" (I John 4:4, italics added). The word greater is a translation of the Greek word, meizon. It is a quantitative word, meaning larger or more. This verse literally means: there is more of God in you than there is evil in the world. This is further supported by what Paul wrote to the church in Ephesus. He said, "Know the love of Christ which surpasses knowledge, that you may be filled up to all the fullness of God" (Ephesians 3:19, italics added). The word "fullness" is a translation of the Greek word, pleroma. It literally means what fills. Paul told the Ephesians that they could be filled with everything that filled God.

With that revelation in mind, a command like "love one another like I love you" does not seem so unrealistic. Loving people like Jesus did is our true nature and capacity. Suddenly, God telling two people (Adam and Eve) to fill the earth, and subdue it and rule it seems quite reasonable. That was their capacity in God. When Jesus told Peter that he should forgive his brother up to 70 times seven, He was not suggesting that after 490 offences, he could be angry and bitter with his brother. Jesus literally meant that Peter had the same capacity for forgiveness that He had.

The need for understanding our spiritual capacities cannot be overstated. It is unlikely that we will believe for, expect and access a supply greater than what we think we have the capacity for. It is not enough to just know how big God is, we need to understand how big God is in each one of us. Winston Churchill captured the spirit of this point when he wrote to his wife Clementine during some enormous challenges in World War I. He said, "I am superior to anything that can happen to me out here." (63) The Biblical record is replete with those who were superior to even the most impossible circumstances. Elijah outrunning a horse for 32 kilometres (I Kings 18:46), and Shadrach, Meshach and Abednego being unharmed in a fiery furnace (Daniel 3:27) attest to the power of this spiritual capacity. From Jesus walking on water (Mark 6:48) to the shadow of Peter healing the sick (Acts 5:15), we witness the limitless possibilities of man's spiritual inheritance.

One example of this limitless inheritance was experienced by one of our younger leaders, Joel Clark. He was the youth pastor at our church in Johannesburg. Quite frankly, it was the sort of miracle I would have expected from someone like Joel. He is one of the most un-religious and out-of-the-box leaders I have ever had the privilege of working with. Joel always does so many creative and cutting-edge things for the sake of young people and the Kingdom.

He was actually on his way to have lunch when it happened. McDonalds had finally arrived in South Africa in the early 1990s, and he was looking forward to a Big Mac attack. As he approached the entrance of the restaurant, he saw a handful of kids coming his way to beg for money. Not feeling particularly altruistic, he quickened his pace to avoid being intercepted by the hungry little mob. Once safely inside, however, he felt the nudge of the Holy Spirit. Joel instantly knew that his Mac attack would have to wait. Looking outside, he counted the number of children at about eight. He was glad to find that he had just enough money for eight cheeseburgers — maybe not Combos, but at least it was something.

As he left McDonalds, with burgers in hand, however, he was suddenly confronted by an unexpected turn of events; the group of children had doubled in size. This was now a problem. In the African context, having more mouths to feed than food to share can often turn disastrous. Things can get ugly. Joel's quick prayer of "Lord, what do I do?" was followed by the Holy Spirit's reassuring voice, "Hand out the burgers."

After pulling the eighth burger from his backpack and giving it away, he decided to reach back in, and to his surprise, there was another and then another, and then another, until every kid got their burger. Out of the Spirit came enough burgers for everyone. This is a small, but vivid illustration of how limitless our capacities are in Him. More of this will be addressed in Chapter Six on Spirit-filled enablement.

Conclusion

In the Sermon on the Mount, Jesus commanded his disciples to pray that the Kingdom would come on earth as it is in heaven (Matthew 6:10). He then followed up that directive with a stark reminder that they should first seek his Kingdom and his righteousness, so that all things would be added (Matthew 6:33). The weight of Scripture supports the premise that the primary focus of apostles and apostolic leadership is to bring the Kingdom of God into all spheres of life. This means declaring and demonstrating the rule of God in all things pertaining to life. In Be a Leader for God's Sake, Professor Bruce Winston, highlighting a leader's pursuit of the Kingdom as their main focus, noted that the word "added" is the Greek word prostithemi, meaning increase or proceed further. (64) Part of that adding or increase, which furthers the progress of the kingdom, is a community of believers (the Church) who are being engaged and equipped by apostles and apostolic leaders.

This relationship between apostles and God's people shapes a culture that is motivated by shared values, grounded in familial relationships, advanced and governed through Biblical partnerships and teams, guided within a global perspective and empowered by the Holy Spirit. Rather than simply depending on a few apostles or apostolic teams, effective transformation stems from a people who have the capacity for the impossible. It is within this environment that prolific leadership development and deployment occurs. In the next chapter, we look at specific values that are critical for developing this leadership culture.

Discussion questions

1.1 What is an apostle?
1.2 Describe several ways in which apostles affect a community of people.
1.3 What does it mean for a community of people to be apostolic?
1.4 How would you describe an apostolic leadership culture?
1.5 What does it mean to bring the Kingdom?
1.6 Identify anything in your life that may hinder you from bringing the Kingdom.
1.7 What are you currently doing that most reflects an apostolic culture?

CHAPTER TWO

The Drive of Values

While arguing the merits of values-based leadership, James O'Toole asked the question, "Can we imagine a situation in which Christ would be successful in winning over the crowd by being tough, abusive and unconcerned with their needs? How far would He get by commanding them to love their neighbours?" (1) The point being: when there is dissonance, i.e. when the really important things (values) and the actions taken by leaders are not in correct alignment, alienation, cynicism and distrust can enter. Although O'Toole is not a practising Christian, he noted that Christianity depended on values-based leadership to "inspire others to lead transformation". (2)

There was a group of leaders that continually harassed Jesus and represented the antithesis of inspiring others towards transformation, namely the Pharisees. Jesus said, "Rightly did Isaiah prophesy of you hypocrites, as it is written, 'This people honours Me with their lips, but their heart is far away from Me'" (Mark 7:6). Jesus went out of his way to expose the folly of leaders who either had the wrong values, or the right values, but without matching behaviour and actions. He chastised the Pharisees, saying that they loved "the place of honour" more than loving God (Matthew 23:6), and He exposed their use of prayer as a pretence for taking money from widows (Matthew 23:14).

The first problem (wrong values) is illustrated in Adam Smith's concept of self-interest. He called self-interest the solitary driver for all individual effort and economic performance. It has led to what Dr Bruce Winston refers to as the "self-love" of commercial enterprises. (3) Instead of the economy being driven by a value for people and a desire to improve the quality of life through service and innovation, we are left with transactional relationships rooted primarily in selfishness.

The second problem (right values/wrong behaviour) becomes glaringly apparent when organisations advocate a noble value such as leadership development, yet continually avoid questions or conversations that may challenge the status quo, or view them as insubordinate. Meaning, the advocated value is not backed up by attitudes and behaviour commensurate with developing leaders. This can lead to an organisational environment rife with discouragement, mistrust and cynicism.

Implicit in the value of developing leaders is the notion of challenging our thinking for the purpose of improvement. When an important value isn't supported by appropriate behaviour and actions, it shows a lack of authenticity. While addressing a theoretical framework for assessing effectiveness and leadership development in Africa, Van Rensburg highlighted authenticity as the fuel for trust, innovation and creativity. (4)

> **When an important value isn't supported by appropriate behaviour and actions, it shows a lack of authenticity.**

During over 30 years of personal leadership experience, I have seen the non-alignment of values and actions produce more leadership fallout and loss than any other single problem relating to leaders and leading. The two problems discussed above highlight the efficacy and causal nature of our values. Identifying, understanding and living one's values are critical components of any leadership relationship. What are values, why are they so important, and which values are most critical for shaping an apostolic culture that will result in effective and sustainable transformation?

The Vitality of Values

Is there anything more catalytic to our human condition than our values? Is there anything that drives attitudes, behaviour and actions more than what we perceive to be important for our health and wellbeing? If the late Milton Rokeach, a leading researcher and scholar on human values, was correct in saying, "Our values provide us with a set of standards to guide us in all our efforts", then the answer is probably "No". (5) Nothing has a greater impact on our livelihood than what we truly value.

40

Lyle Schaller called values the single most important element of any corporate, congregational or denominational culture. (6) In *Values Driven Leadership*, Aubrey Malphurs referred to values as the driving force behind attitudes, behaviour and actions. (7) They determine our distinctiveness, inspire our efforts and anchor our resolve. The writer of Proverbs described this driving force as an individual's "heart" or the inner region

Nothing has a greater impact on our livelihood than what we truly value.

from where the issues of life spring forth (Proverbs 4:23). The Hebrew word for heart means the centre of anything or the core of what we think, feel and care for. It is the essence of who we are and what we deem as important and valuable.

In their seminal work, *The Leadership Challenge*, Jim Kouzes and Barry Posner define the process of clarifying one's values as "finding your voice". They said, "To find your voice (values) you have to explore your inner territory. You have to take a journey into those places in your heart and soul where you bury your treasures ..." (8) When Jesus said, "Where your treasure is, there your heart will be also" (Matthew 6:20), He was equating our treasures, or what we greatly value, with our core nature and drive.

This spiritual heart, or what I call our values organ, is as essential to leadership as the physical heart is to the human body. Just as our physical heart drives vital nutrients via the blood to and through all parts of the body, so too, the spiritual heart, the centre of who we are and what we are passionate about, is responsible for what goes in and out of our lives, relationships and organisations. Malphurs amplified this point by calling our values the basis for all behaviour, the bottom line for what we will or will not do. (9)

Taking this metaphor of the human heart one step further, we could say, for example, that if the heart is hampered in moving blood to various parts of the body, death can occur. Equally true, when what we deeply value cannot be realised through appropriate behaviour and actions, a type of death can invade our personal lives and relationships. How many dreams and visions have died through lack of faith and hope? How many marriages have died because there was no true intimacy? How many relationships have been lost because humility and honesty were absent? How much trust has been vanquished because honour and respect are an endangered species? The answer to that may be more than any leader cares to admit.

When the human body is well nourished, exercised and rested, which are the core values for bodily health, a healthy state is the normal outcome. When it is not, sickness and disease usually occur. In similar fashion, values that are understood, shared and modelled become a source of health and wellbeing within a community, while values that aren't shared and experienced can become a recipe for broken relationships and dysfunctional organisations.

In South Africa, many Christians and their churches have a passion for social justice. Values such as equality and unity are a significant driving force for behaviour and strategy. For example, helping the poor and disadvantaged through development programmes, or facilitating reconciliation between previously estranged ethnic groups or communities. It is more than just one preference in a sea of philanthropic options. In the South African context, equality is motivated by Christian conscience, a deep empathy for people and African communalistic culture.

Churches such as Rhema and His People Church in Johannesburg are fully integrated, socially relevant and thriving. Most of these socially relevant churches would struggle to exist, if they didn't model these values. Historically, people have left churches and broken fellowship because of the incongruity between the value of equality and the policies of organisations supporting discrimination.

The theological support of apartheid by the Dutch Reformed Church (DRC) of South Africa, which separated Christian brothers and sisters into racial categories, resulted in enormous personal, relational and organisational casualties. DRC leaders who renounced apartheid, such as Dr Beyers Naudé, were declared heretics and repudiated by their own family and friends. It caused tens of thousands of South Africans to give up their personal safety and security as they resisted a system diametrically opposed to their values and convictions. The current peace in South Africa is due, at least in part, to a stronger alignment between the actions of government and the heartfelt beliefs and values of the majority of South Africans.

The apostolic ministry of the Apostle Paul is a stark reminder of how values and core beliefs should be reflected through the behaviour and actions of leaders. In his letter to the Galatians, Paul refers to his rebuke of Peter, who had treated the Gentiles dishonourably, in order to appease the Judaizers in the church. The core value highlighted by Paul to the church in Galatia, namely "For you are all one in Christ Jesus" (Galatians 3:28), was clearly violated by Peter's shunning of the Gentile believers.

Kouzes and Posner made it an issue of credibility when they said, "When it comes to deciding whether a leader is believable; people first listen to the words; they then watch the action. They listen to the talk and watch the walk. Then they measure the congruence. A judgment of 'credible' is handed down when the two are consonant." (10)

Many years ago, at His People Church in Johannesburg, South Africa, our leadership team was confronted with a stark mismatch between a specific church value and what was being modelled among our leaders. We soon discovered that, in spite of possessing a multigenerational core value and having a fair number of senior citizens in the church, there was no one on the senior leadership team above the age of 45. We quickly remedied the situation with some elderly affirmative

Author Danny Silk argues that the presence of God and the worship of God are the top priorities of the apostle.

action. This issue of aligning actions with shared values was a critical part of how Connie and I grafted into our relationships and leadership roles in South Africa.

From the earliest days of our ministry until now, the apostolic value of knowing God and making Him known has defined Connie and I as a couple. I refer to this as an apostolic value because God's presence being realised in all of life is the priority of apostles and apostolic leaders. Jesus said that knowing God was the real measure of eternal life (John 17:3), and Paul called knowing Jesus Christ, the "surpassing value" (Philippians 3:8). In his thought-provoking book *Culture of Honor* pastor and author Danny Silk argues that the presence of God and the worship of God are the top priorities of the apostle. He said, "Apostolic leaders are focused on heaven, and their mission is to see heaven's supernatural reality established on the earth." (11)

Cannistraci supports this assertion by calling intimacy with Jesus Christ a chief requirement of any apostle or apostolic leader. (12) From our church-planting efforts in the United States and South Africa to the very nature of our relationships, knowing God personally and powerfully has shaped our life journey. The presence of this value has added meaning, motivation and definition to over 30 years of full-time Christian service.

Whether starting campus ministries, planting churches or partnering with other like-minded believers and leaders, certain values and their corresponding actions have meant the difference between success and failure in our lives. In fact, in the South African context, they inoculated our hearts against certain survivor instincts that can become quite viral in times of crisis. For example, when South Africa seemed to be slipping towards anarchy, just prior to the 1994 elections, and some individuals and ministries were seeking more secure havens overseas, our value for God and the people prevented us from considering any such avenue. In their 1992 article, entitled Values and the American Manager, Barry Posner and Warren Schmidt wrote that in times of turbulence, values provide connection and direction amid conflicting demands and pressures. (13) Kuczmarski and Kuczmarski, in Values-Based Leadership, defined this as the "bonding power for individuals in a group". (14) Of course, Jesus just called it loving others as He loved us (John 13:34), while Paul referred to it as considering others more important than ourselves (Philippians 2:3).

In spite of South Africa's turbulence and trauma, shared values like trust and community helped shape our redemptive vision and proactive strategies. When others saw only chaos and personal loss, we saw a nation filled with God's people who were being empowered and equipped to bless a continent. Unfortunately for many, the apartheid system did create an environment that valued separation and survival more than co-operation and progress — hardly a favourable setting for developing an apostolic leadership culture. By understanding the role and impact of kingdom values shared within a community of believers, we were able to take a big step towards shaping such a culture.

Values, the Apostolic and Transformation

Dr Bruce Winston describes the Beatitudes as a compilation of heart standards or "values" representing the most significant internal motivators and drivers for leadership behaviour and actions. (15) His statement that "leadership starts with values" is evident in the way Jesus developed his first team of leaders. (16) While preparing his early disciples for their future ministries, Jesus' first priority was to lay a foundation of values that was suitable to their apostolic leadership roles. By emphasising specific values before behaviour and strategies, Jesus established a priority standard for all future apostles and apostolic ministry.

According to Dr Winston, values such as humility, self-control, integrity, truth, mercy and peace were fundamental to the apostles' leadership development and efforts. In other words, specific values are the basis of other essential apostolic characteristics and behaviour. Even the fundamental leadership quality known as "forward-looking" finds origin and traction in the values and desires of the heart.

> **Jesus' first priority was to lay a foundation of values that was suitable to their apostolic leadership roles.**

Kouzes and Posner pointed out that most people who take on a leadership role do not start with a clear vision of the future. They describe the process of finding vision as a "deeply emotional and intuitive exercise", i.e. what you care about or what you value determines your capacity to envision a specific future. (17) The Beatitudes imply that before Jesus' first apostles could realise a better tomorrow, they needed values or drivers capable of acquiring it.

In *The Fifth Discipline*, Peter Senge took it a step further when he wrote, "A vision not consistent with values that people live by day to day will not only fail to inspire genuine enthusiasm, it will often foster outright cynicism." (18) Put simply, the authenticity of a vision requires values that are equal to the task. For example, there have been times, while doing marriage counselling, that Connie and I found it difficult to see much of a future for the hopeful couple because values like friendship, humility, serving and self-control were not present. This causal relationship between values and the vision is noteworthy.

American leaders like Thomas Jefferson, Abraham Lincoln and Theodore Roosevelt approached their vision of an "equal-opportunity" America through the lens of values-based leadership. It was their understanding of sustained and shared commitment to "fundamental values", rather than "ephemeral details" that would turn the ambitious values of "life, liberty and the pursuit of happiness" into a better tomorrow for all Americans. (19)

> **The authenticity of a vision requires values that are equal to the task.**

45

It took shared values such as freedom, equality and justice shaping new ethical behaviour and strategies (Rustenburg Accord and the Congress for the Democratisation of South Africa), before the vision of a fully democratic South Africa could be realised. This values-driven approach appears to be at the core of apostolic leadership. Interestingly, Jesus used the disciples' debate over who was the greatest to refute the paternalism of Gentile kings and promote leadership that is vested in such values as humility and servanthood (Luke 22:25–26). He made a distinction between those who practised traditional command and controlled leadership, according to the adage, "power, purpose and privilege resides with those at the top", and leaders who valued "others and service" more than personal gain. (20)

In his book, *Leading Change*, O'Toole argues that leading from inspirational values is in sharp contrast to the more prescriptive leadership approaches. He writes, "Effective leaders must begin by setting aside the culturally conditioned natural instinct to lead by push, particularly when times are tough. Leaders must instead adopt the unnatural behaviour of always leading by the pull of inspiring values." (21)

Leading by the pull of inspiring values is more than just optional for developing an apostolic leadership culture. When Paul was defending his apostleship to the church in Corinth, he refused to boast in the position or authority given to him by God. Instead, he said, "Consider this, what we are in word by letters when absent, we are also in deed when we are present" (2 Corinthians 10:11). This means that our authority is evident, not in our position, but in the alignment of the values and beliefs we teach, and the lives we model.

> **Our authority is evident, not in our position, but in the alignment of the values and beliefs we teach, and the lives we model.**

When leaving Timothy in Ephesus as a delegated apostolic leader, Paul mirrored this values-driven model. Timothy was charged by Paul to be an example of "love, faith and purity" to all who believe (1 Timothy 4:12). In other words, Timothy could have the best influence as a leader by modelling specific values, rather than exercising positional authority. Is it any wonder that the lion's share of qualifications for an elder, as highlighted by Paul, is based on character?

46

Van Rensburg attributes sustainable positive influence in Africa to the "modelling of character and integrity". (22) The dedication of his book *The Leadership Challenge in Africa* to Archbishop Desmond Tutu reflects the strength of that conviction. Leaders like Desmond Tutu embody Paul's charge to seek what is good for all people by pursuing values like faith, love and peace (I Thessalonians 5:15 and 2 Timothy 2:22).

This values-based approach engenders a transformational ethos for both the apostolic leader and any subsequent relationships. Transformation is defined as the change in form, appearance, nature or character of something, while ethos is the character or disposition of a person, group or community. A transformational ethos is when a person or a people are poised for change. In his extensive work *The Leadership Experience* Richard Daft noted that transformational leadership is based on the values and beliefs of a leader, rather than on an exchange process between leader and follower, and is characterised by an ability to bring about significant and sustainable change. (23)

Rather than being driven by the "self-interest common to transactional relationships", or dependent upon the "charisma of individual leaders", values-driven, apostolic leadership is motivated by transcendent values determined by God, and discovered and shared within a community of believers. It elevates leaders and followers beyond self-interest towards a desired future state. (24)

When the disciples reminded Jesus that they had left everything to follow Him, He said, "There is no one who has left house or brothers or sisters or mother or father or children or farms, for My sake and for the gospel's sake, but that he will receive a hundred times as much now in the present age ... and in the age to come" (Mark 10:29–30). In other words, as they lived the values of the kingdom, a brighter future for all was guaranteed. According to author Leighton Ford in *Transforming Leadership*, an environment for significant change is created by raising

> **The declaration and application of heaven in all spheres of life, is sown and grown in a values-driven, transformational environment.**

awareness of certain values and transcending the restraints of self-interest. (25) Paul's exhortation to the Roman Christians amplified the nature of this change, as well as the efficacy of kingdom values. He said that renewing their minds would produce a transformation that resulted in proving the perfect will of God (Romans 12:2).

The kingdom mandate given to apostolic leadership, which is the declaration and application of heaven in all spheres of life, is sown and grown in a values-driven, transformational environment. A critical next step is the discovery and application of specific kingdom values.

There are a host of values that will motivate and shape an apostolic leadership culture, such as repentance, faith, humility, serving, excellence, giving, creativity, innovation, vision, diversity, unity, worship, prayer, evangelism, discipleship and community. In almost every epistle that Paul wrote, he highlighted these core drivers and kingdom focuses. In Romans 12, he linked transformation and proving the perfect will of God to values of faith, grace, serving, teaching, giving, leading, mercy, respect and peace.

In emphasising the prominence of the Holy Spirit, Paul motivated the Galatians with the values of love, joy, peace, patience, kindness, goodness, faithfulness, gentleness and self-control (Galatians 5:22–23). To the church in Corinth, he promoted drivers such as faith, hope, love, wisdom, healing, miracles and honour, while to the Ephesians, he emphasised purpose, redemption, revelation, identity, inheritance, unity and relationships.

Although many values will make up an apostolic culture, only a few are critical to the rest. Milton Rokeach identified two main types of values: "ends values" and "means values". (26) The former are "ultimate end-states of existence worth striving for" such as knowing God, while the latter are "modes of behaviour" to attain the end state such as prayer and learning. (27) Rokeach argued that there are a small number of ends values that

> **There are two values more fundamental and catalytic than any other for developing an apostolic leadership culture.**

were ordered or organised in countless ways, i.e. there were a few values that caused a multitude of leadership attitudes, and behaviour and actions.

That said, there are two values more fundamental and catalytic than any other for developing an apostolic leadership culture. Jesus revealed these two essential values when He declared the greatest commandments: "You shall love the Lord your God with all your heart, and with all your soul, and with all your mind" and "You shall love your neighbour as yourself" (Matthew 22:37–39). How we approach God and others has a provocative impact on all aspects of the apostolic culture. It's an approach rooted in divine revelation and lived out through behaviour and practices corresponding to valuing others and knowing God.

Values Origin, People and God

Firstly, addressing the origin of values, Geisler and Feinberg argued, "Values, for the Christian, are determined by God and disclosed by revelation to man." (28) The fact that certain values have transcendent existence cannot be overstated. When Paul told the Philippians to dwell on "whatever is true, whatever is honorable,

> **The Creator decides and the created discovers.**

whatever is right, whatever is pure, whatever is [a]lovely, whatever is of good repute, if there is any excellence and if anything worthy of praise" (Philippians 4:8), he was prioritising the disclosure and discovery of fundamental values. He reminded them that what they had "learned and received and heard and seen" in him (Philippians 4:9), he had received by way of revelation from the Lord.

Although the discovery of values is the domain and responsibility of every individual, it is imperative that there is no confusion surrounding the first cause of fundamental value or values. From a theistic worldview or an apostolic perspective, the axiological question, or, what is the ultimate value, is answered as, "God is the ultimate value and what He values is of value." (29) In other words, fundamental value is not created by man any more than what right or wrong is. As author and teacher Graham Cook succinctly noted, "The Creator decides and the created discovers."

God has set the value for all people by virtue of his creation. In Genesis 1:26, God said, "Let Us make man in Our image, according to Our likeness." Therefore, mankind, being created by God with unique existence, has independent value. Man's ultimate value is intrinsic; it does not depend upon finite behaviour and actions. In addressing the concept of human value and civil government, authors Steve McDowell and Mark Beliles said, "His value is not dependent upon his ability to contribute to the state. Man is the highest value and the state exists to serve

49

man." (31) Therefore, people should never be treated as a means to another end. Being valuable precedes doing valuable things.

Gerard van Rensburg describes South Africa's "better leaders", or those best suited to addressing the challenges of transformation in South Africa, as being anchored in "values that respect the uniqueness of the individual ..." (32) Unlike utilitarianism, which defines value as the greatest happiness for the greatest number of people, or pragmatism, which, according to Dr Glen Martin, advocates a relative truth, where value is determined by the most rational choice at any given moment, human value is a constant at all times and under all circumstances. When the divine origin of human value is missing, we are left with Siberian Gulags, Nazi concentration camps, Rwandan genocides, rampant abortion and South African apartheid.

From the South African context, Archbishop Desmond Tutu put it rather poignantly when he said, "The white minority used a system of 'pigmentocracy' to claim that what invested human beings with worth (value) was a particular skin colour, ethnicity and race." He continued, "What endows human beings, every single human being without exception, with infinite worth is not this or that biological or any other external attribute. No, it is the fact that each one of us has been created in the image of God." (33)

We are honoured at birth by being made in His image.

When human value is seen through the eyes of divine origin, humanity reaps the benefits of leaders like Mother Teresa, Martin Luther King Jr. and Nelson Mandela. When it is not, it produces Ivan the Terrible, Stalin, Mao Tse-tung, Hitler, Pol Pot and Saddam Hussein. The issue of recognising, receiving and releasing the value of another person, which is a ubiquitous feature of an apostolic leadership culture, is grounded in Jesus' command to love one another just as He loves us (John 13), and is expressed through a concept known as honour.

To honour another person is the act of recognising and receiving their value or worth. It goes far beyond mere compliments, the demonstration of appreciation or the recognition of accomplishments. As Fawn Parish noted, "We are honoured at birth by being made in His image." (34) The Greek word for honour, timao, means to highly esteem, to prize, to give weight to, to ascribe worth. It is literally the degree of value that we attribute to something or someone.

When Jesus said, "He who receives a prophet in the name of a prophet shall receive a prophet's reward" (Matthew 10:41), He revealed the efficacy of honouring someone. Giving honour to someone became a conduit for receiving their unique contribution. In fact, it was recorded that Jesus' own ability to do miracles in Nazareth was significantly hindered by the lack of honour coming from the townsfolk (Mark 6:4–5). Our ability to receive from God and others is linked to the giving and receiving of honour.

At the baptism of Jesus, the audible voice of the Father was heard saying, "You are My beloved Son, in You I am well-pleased" (Luke 3:22). Before Jesus began his ministry, before He made one disciple or performed one miracle, the Father honoured (valued) Him as a son full of his pleasure. The Father's announcement confirmed that the worth ascribed to an individual precedes their performance. This is no way diminishes the importance of someone's behaviour or labours, but it affirms that a person's value is first about who they are before it is what they do.

This intrinsic value or honour is not just reserved for a select few. Peter's admonition to "honour all people" (1 Peter 2:17) levels the playing field to include everyone; not just the gifted, successful and powerful. In *The Power of Honor*, author Fawn Parish made a provocative observation when she wrote, "If honour was the basis of how we thought and acted toward one another, imagine the possibilities. If we began to regard each other with the significance that God Himself regards us, imagine how life would change." (35) She noted that much

> **Recognising a person's intrinsic value as the apex of God's creation is the best catalyst for releasing treasureshidden in every human life.**

of our honour today is based on merit and benchmarked by the accomplishments of others. Therefore, many people never enjoy the benefits of expressing and receiving honour that is both intrinsic from God and extrinsic from man. In fact, recognising a person's intrinsic value as the apex of God's creation is the best catalyst for releasing treasures hidden in every human life.

There are few things that open the treasury of the human soul as quickly as a leader who shows sincere interest and concern for others. It is one thing to employ the head and hands of someone's competence and skill, but gaining the heart, the deepest level of a person's passion and capacity, comes through the recognition of their personal worth. Dr Winston argues that today's employees want to be considered for their hearts, as well as their hands; for who they are and not just for what they do. He said that by practising love in an organisation, people become "hired hearts" and not just "hired hands". (36)

It is worth noting that, soon after Jesus lovingly ministered to Mary Magdalene at a Pharisee's house, Mary began travelling with Jesus and supporting Him from her personal means (Luke 7 and 8).

After one of our leaders from His People Church in Johannesburg, David Webb, had picked me up from the airport one day, we were discussing some of the pitfalls of command and control leadership in the car on the way home. He told me how surprised he'd been by all the honour and freedom he was given when he first arrived as a new leader on our leadership team. Honestly, in my mind, there was nothing exceptional about his experience.

The first thing we should always give someone who God adds to our team, or even our church, is honour and respect. The recognition of personal value begins at the door, and not with the job description. Showing honour and respect is a natural by-product of our heartfelt belief that each person is special and unique, and will make us better people. Knowing someone on a life journey is infinitely more powerful than any ministry accomplishment.

Addressing the issue of honour in *Loving on Purpose*, veteran pastor/counsellor Danny Silk says that honour is a two-way experience where free people can remain powerful in a relationship. He says that, when we violate another person's need for value, "dishonour rushes in and fills our motivations with fear." (37) When our behaviour and actions are driven by fear, we live in survivor mode; we make choices for the purpose of acceptance and safety, rather than change and progress.

When we violate another person's need for value, dishonour rushes in and fills our motivations with fear.

Jesus said that, because of fear, people "were subject to slavery all their lives" (Hebrews 2:15). How many leadership teams are a slave-ship rather than an apostleship? How many good leaders have jumped ship, simply to escape the smothering atmosphere of fear and intimidation? There are few things as stifling to a leadership culture as the spirit of fear, and few things more favourable to fostering fear than rampant dishonour within a community of people.

When Paul wrote, "Therefore from now on we recognise no man according to the flesh," (2 Corinthians 15:16), he revealed a key to cultivating a culture of honour. This thought was placed in the context of, "For the love of Christ controls us" (2 Corinthians 15:14). In other words, our attitudes and actions towards someone should not be determined by anything other than how they are viewed from heaven. Rather than being defined by single events, personal shortcomings or organisational strategies, each life should be seen through the lens of "For you formed my inward parts; you wove me in my mother's womb ... I am fearfully and wonderfully made" (Psalm 139:13–14).

This is not about turning a blind eye to human weakness or personal inadequacy; rather, it's about approaching every human life from God's perspective. The wonderful works of God are in every individual, and the discovery of those wonderful works is determined, to a large extent, by the amount of honour given and received in relationships. Graham Cooke calls it focusing on what is noble in people, so that nobility can emerge. (38) This culture of honour is driven by another essential value common to an apostolic leadership culture: the primacy of knowing God and his goodness.

Knowing God's Goodness

Bobby Connor from Eagles View Ministries suggests that many Christians are far too familiar with a God they hardly know, i.e. the language that Christians use to describe the quality of their relationship with God is seldom backed by real sacrifice and experience. While they may declare quite passionately and articulately that Jesus is the saviour,

> **Many Christians are far too familiar with a God they hardly know.**

healer, deliverer, counsellor and provider, the evidence of those benefits is lacking not only in their personal lives, but also in their actions towards others.

In *Passion for Jesus*, author Mike Bickle called this an "inadequate understanding of the heart of God". (39) He said the greatest need of the hour was for the true knowledge of God; a knowledge that goes beyond the mere "studying of words on paper". (40) Jesus highlighted this dichotomy when He admonished the Pharisees as follows, "You search the Scriptures because you think that in them you have eternal life; it is these that testify about Me; and you are unwilling to come to Me so that you may have life" (John 5:39–40, italics added). Bickle goes on to say, "The great need of the Church is to see, know and discover the indescribable glory of who God is." (41)

Cannistraci noted that the apostles of the New Testament moved in great power and wielded enormous influence because of their intimacy with God. He went on to say that elevated intimacy with God would characterise the emerging apostolic movement. (42) Few apostolic leaders reflected this attribute as unmistakably and poignantly as Paul. He said, "[For my determined purpose is] that I may know Him [that I may progressively become more deeply and intimately acquainted with Him, perceiving and recognising and understanding the wonders of His Person more strongly and more clearly]" (Philippians 3:10, Amplified).

> **The great need of the Church is to see, know and discover the indescribable glory of who God is.**

Lest anyone view this as a unique standard for a select group of apostles, Paul reminded the Ephesians that they were all called "to know the love of Christ" that they may "be filled up to all the fullness of God" (Ephesians 3:19). Although all of God's attributes are amazing and provocative, one that stands out as catalytic to the rest is his goodness. Mike Bickle called God's goodness the basis for all blessings.

In his work *The Knowledge of the Holy* A.W.Tozer called God's goodness the ground for all our expectations. Tozer acknowledged the importance of repentance, faith and human effort, but he placed no confidence in anything but the "goodness of God". He said, "The whole outlook of Mankind might be changed if we could all believe that we dwell under a friendly sky." (43) Put another way, God is not mad at anyone, sinner or saint.

Apostolic leader and author Bill Johnson echoed this sentiment by describing God's goodness as the "cornerstone of revelation". (44) He said that the bedrock of right (faith) response under any circumstances was the "burning conviction that

God is good, always good". (45) The nature of God's goodness is so comprehensive that Paul told the Romans that God causes "all things to work together for good" (Romans 8:28). The Greek word for good is agathos, meaning benevolent, profitable and useful. In other words, in the widest sense, God's intentions towards his people are always good. A true apostolic culture reflects what Paul declared to the Philippians: "We ... glory

> **The bedrock of right (faith) response under any circumstances is the "burning conviction that God is good, always good**

in Christ Jesus and put no confidence in the flesh" (Philippians 3:3). He told the Philippians that the very thing he was confident of was God's goodness at work in them (Philippians 1:6). That goodness is summed up in the nature of God's saving grace towards humanity.

One of the most quoted verses from the Bible is John 3:16, which reads, "For God so loved the world, that He gave His only begotten Son ..." Through Jesus, God's entire disposition towards the human race is one of love, for the purpose of everyone's wellbeing. Jesus said that He did not come to judge, but to save.

The apostle Peter stated unequivocally that God did not want anyone "to perish but for all to come to repentance" (2 Peter 3:9). Likewise, Bill Johnson referred to repentance as gaining "God's perspective of reality". (46) The Father's sole agenda is to lead everyone into the reality of his salvation.

When James and John sought permission to apply Old Testament judgment on some inhospitable Samaritans by calling fire down from heaven, Jesus retorted, "The Son of Man did not come to destroy ... but to save" (Luke 9:56).

The Greek word for save is sozo, and it means to save, heal, deliver, preserve, make whole, or to preserve safe from danger, loss or destruction. It means salvation in a comprehensive sense. To know God's goodness is to experience the extensive nature of his salvation first-hand. It begins with the belief that God desires to save, deliver and heal everyone. Bill Johnson makes an interesting observation: he says that if we believe that it's not the will of God to heal everyone, we will begin cutting ourselves off from releasing faith in that area. John confirmed this point when he wrote, "This is the confidence which we have before Him, that, if we ask anything according to His will, He hears us. And if we know that He hears us ... we know that we have the requests ..." (1 John 5:14–15, italics added).

What is true in the area of sickness and disease is equally true for every human issue. Our faith, which rests in the nature and will of God, operates within the parameters of what we believe to be his character and desire. Herein lies the most critical aspect of developing an apostolic leadership culture: having the revelation of God's goodness "to reconcile all things to Himself ... whether things on earth or things in heaven" (Colossians 1:20). Cannistraci refers to this as one of the earmarks of an apostolic people, where entire cultures can be impacted by the saving, healing and delivering power of God's goodness.

Although most Christians acknowledge God as being good, this goodness is all too often defined as, what God does in response to what we do. Meaning, his goodness is generated towards us because of our goodness. For example, because we repent (good), He forgives (good); or, because we pray (good), He provides (good). This transactional approach to God's goodness is one of the most insidious deceptions about the character of God, and it diminishes a confident access to his mercy and grace.

> **This transactional approach to God's goodness is one of the most insidious deceptions about the character of God, and it diminishes a confident access to his mercy and grace.**

Of course, good decisions position us to receive, but his goodness has already been poured out. When Jesus said that God "sends rain on the righteous and unrighteous" alike (Matthew 5:45), He was highlighting this aspect of his goodness. It means shifting from living to obtain his goodness, to living from his goodness.

Prior to becoming a Christian, I learned this wonderful lesson the hard way. I was a university student, and blindly indulging all my carnal desires. I was at a party and recklessly consuming various quantities of illegal drugs when, suddenly, I found myself in the paralysing fear of an overdose. I was convulsing terribly and looking to my friends for assistance. Their solution to my predicament was to abandon me. In that moment, accompanied by nothing but the dread of my mortality, I had a sudden memory: a real blast from the past. I remembered my great-grandmother Margaret Klinger. Interestingly, she was the only real Christian that I was aware of in our entire extended family.

She was long gone by then, having passed away when I was a young boy, but the memory of her on her knees praying at her bedside was being projected into my mind. She was the Jesus freak that people made funny remarks about. I would sometimes stay overnight at her house and witness these strange Christian ways. Sadly, while she was off in her room praying to Jesus to save my dark little soul, I would be taking money from her purse.

Now, many years later, in a terrifying, drug-induced state, her prayer to this Jesus that I didn't know gained traction in my thoughts. The only prayer I could muster was, "Jesus, if you are real, can you help me?" As soon as the last word left my mouth, I felt a thick, warm liquid pour over me. It started on my head and moved all the way down to my feet. By the time it had moved through my body, I was healed of the overdose and in my right mind.

I am driven and motivated by and from his goodness, rather than for it.

It wasn't until much later that I became a Christian, but that was the moment when I discovered something amazing about God's goodness. He had put that thought into my mind. His goodness was at work way before I could do anything good. As a result, I am driven and motivated by and from his goodness, rather than for it.

Conclusion

James McGregor Burns calls values the "hypersensitive force field of motivation". (47) Deep-seated beliefs and values are the motivating force behind most leadership behaviour and actions. Sharing values within a specific community of people becomes the foundational thrust for building productive and genuine relationships.

While the discovery of values is the responsibility of every individual, it is incumbent upon leaders to understand the provocative nature of values; to identify, build and affirm shared values, and to align corresponding actions with those shared values. Everything, from the quality of the vision to the extent of effective transformation, will be driven by certain kingdom values. In other words, our value for God and others determines the quality of our relationships, as well as the nature of our transformational efforts in civil society.

Of course, there are few things as provocative to this end as a life-changing encounter with the goodness of God. In Chapter Three, we will examine a category of relationships that are most reflective of these values, and most conducive to the apostolic leadership culture.

Discussion questions

2.1 What is a value? What is a core value?

2.2 Consider some of your fundamental values, and give some examples of your corresponding behaviours or actions (behaviours or actions that reflect these values).

2.3 Now give some examples of any possible behaviours or actions that may contradict or conflict with your values.

2.4 Do you lead from the pull of inspiring values? If so, how do you know this?

2.5 How are the concepts of honour and value related?

2.6 Why would the value of God's goodness be so crucial in an apostolic culture?

2.7 What current behaviours or actions best reflect valuing others?

2.8 What does the goodness of God look like in your life and ministry?

CHAPTER THREE

Relationally Grounded

What came first, the chicken or the egg? Well, the chicken, of course! Science has finally caught up with the Bible's account of creation. British scientists used a super computer called HECTOR to examine the finer details of an egg shell. They discovered that a protein, which is only found in chickens, was the catalyst for the shell's formation. (1)

In the same way that a chicken is essential for the creation of an egg, specific relationships are indispensable in fostering an apostolic culture. Even when a relationship is initiated around a specific role, mission or goal, the relationship is still the primary context and conduit for accomplishing the objectives. While describing "the Church that God had in mind", Erwin McManus noted, "An apostolic ethos erupts out of the context of human relationships, not apart from it." (2)

> **An apostolic ethos erupts out of the context of human relationships, not apart from it.**

Jesus echoed these sentiments when He highlighted the power of agreement. He said, "For where two or three have gathered together in My name, I am there in their midst" (Matthew 18:20). The nature of the Kingdom is grounded in God's involvement in our lives through the friendship, fellowship and partnership of other believers.

Veteran Bible teacher Dick Iverson describes relationships as the basis for all spiritual authority, and says that it is by developing healthy relationships that one qualifies for leadership. (3) The relational character of leadership is arguably one of the most prolific and detailed themes modelled in Scripture. From Adam and Eve in the garden, to the ministry of Jesus and the apostles, to present-day communities of faith in civil society, God's design for the expansion of his Kingdom is found within the function of human relationships.

For Jesus, those relationships meant laying down his life for people (John 10:15). The Apostle Paul referred to it as "being rooted and grounded in love" (Ephesians 3:17), while the Apostle Peter described it as remaining fervent in our love for one another (I Peter 4:8). A true apostolic leadership culture not only grows from a leader's friendship with God, but also develops through Bible-based, familial relationships. This chapter will look at the nature of those relationships, as well as the apostolic role of fathering and the significance of multigenerational partnerships.

In *Leadership and the New Science*, author and educator Margaret Wheatley addresses the change from reductionist thinking to holistic thinking. It's where the focus has shifted from the basic building blocks of matter to relationships between discrete parts. She says the machine models of work have given way to the "deep longings we have for community, meaning, dignity and love in our organisational lives". (4) Instead of specific functions, roles and goals, the relationships themselves are now part of this new science insight for leadership.

> **The quality of who we are together is the priority and the basis for new things.**

The African cultural ethic of Ubuntu reflects this relation-oriented approach. It comes from a Xhosa proverb that means, "A person is a person through other persons." (5) It's where the relationship itself becomes the primary focus for growth and productivity. The quality of who we are together is the priority and the basis for new things. For example, even before a new Bafana Bafana soccer star emerges, the parent places a little ball at the feet of their child, who simply kicks it back. This simple action becomes a relational process. The nature of the individuals and their relational connection are the first cause in the discovery of a successful soccer player. Simply put, the character of the relationship is the amino acids for destiny; not job descriptions, strategies or goals.

60

In Ephesians 4:15–16, Paul reminded the church in Ephesus that the joints (relationships) supply "according to the proper working of each individual part". A joint is simply a deep-tissue relationship between two or more parts. Rather than diminishing the significance of a goal or task, this relational approach is a better guarantee for accomplishing the mission, as well as for people to be more like Him and healthier at the end of the journey.

The unparalleled accomplishments of the Jesuits reflect this relational narrative. Former Jesuit and business consultant Chris Lowney says, "Love was the glue that unified the Jesuit Company, a motivating force that energised their efforts." (6) Their relational strength came from what Lowney calls "love-driven leadership". (7) By approaching their relationships through the lens of love, Lowney says the Jesuits had: 1) the vision to see each person's talent, potential and dignity; 2) the courage, passion and commitment to unlock that potential; and 3) the resulting loyalty and mutual support that energises and supports the team.

This love-driven leadership provides the basis for relationships that are more suitable for developing an apostolic culture. While addressing strategic shifts in the 21st century church, Mark Conner noted that churches and ministries were known more for their activities and events than the quality of their relationships. He said, "For too long, church has become a thing we do, an event or an experience, rather than a community of people networked together in loving relationships." (8)

When an individual or a relationship is processed solely through the lens of organisational events, systems and goals, or by the agenda and preferences of a select few, then agreement and conformity become the highest value. Richard Daft refers to this form of leadership as producing people who mindlessly follow orders. He says it diminishes confidence, commitment, enthusiasm, imagination and motivation. (9) When leading with love, however, the uniqueness of individuals and their relationships remain a priority, generating unity and real transformation.

When someone is valued as a person

> **When an individual or a relationship is processed solely through the lens of organisational events, systems and goals, or by the agenda and preferences of a select few, then agreement and conformity become the highest value.**

and given a sense of meaning and contribution to a community (fulfilling the higher needs of heart, mind and body), they tend to give all they have to offer. Jesus said, "By this all men will know that you are My disciples, if you have love for one another" (John 13:35). This love is key evidence that God is at work among a community of people.

Revivalist and author John Crowder calls love the greatest miracle and "the absolute key to walking in power". (10) Few relational models reflect this love behaviour like familial relationships in the Body of Christ, and few reflect it as clearly as the role of fathering.

The Familial and Fathering

The significance of a family and a father seems beyond dispute. Besides the obviousness of human reproduction, the correlation between a father's presence and a family's welfare is notable. Study after study has made links between a father's absence and the likelihood of a child becoming a dropout, jobless, an addict, a victim of suicide, mentally ill or a target of child abuse. (11)

In *Life without Father*, David Popenoe presents compelling evidence supporting the essential role of fatherhood in society. He shows how the negative consequences of fatherlessness are affecting children, women and men everywhere. Popenoe says the damage to children has accumulated to near tidal-wave proportions, and that fatherless children experience significantly more physical, emotional and behavioural problems than children growing up in intact families. (12)

The pandemic of street gangs, crime, drug addiction and sexually transmitted diseases are all attributed to this driving force of fatherlessness.

David Blankenhorn, the founder and president of the Institute for American Values, called fatherlessness "the most harmful demographic of this generation." (13) Addressing the problem of fatherlessness in South Africa, columnist Heidi Holland described the lack of fathers as having left many of the nation's youth "devoid of a conscience." (14) Drawing from an article by the South African Association of Jungian Analysts, she wrote, "We are a fatherless society where many men procreate but lack the capacity to be a father to their children, having come from families in which their own fathers were often either abusive or absent."

The pandemic of street gangs, crime, drug addiction and sexually transmitted diseases are all attributed to this driving force of fatherlessness. To prevent an even greater disaster in the future, community-based organisations are demonstrating improved leadership foresight by implementing more familial-based strategies. Some, like the Masiphane projects in Johannesburg, South Africa, are following the Psalmist's pronouncement, "God makes a home for the lonely" (Psalm 68:6), by focusing on adoptions and other home-based initiatives.

Amazing leaders like David and Caroline Webb are among those who are leading the charge for family-based care. Through their many projects, such as Baby Haven and Child Haven, they have raised the benchmark from orphan care, en masse, to family care with a mom and a dad. They model God becoming "a father of the fatherless" (Psalm 68:5) through the familial nature of the Church and community. James describes caring for widows and the fatherless as "pure and undefiled religion" (James 1:27). This highlights the priority that God places on people accessing family-type support, whether it be a natural family (by birth, marriage or adoption) or a spiritual family (the new birth and Christian community). Unfortunately, spiritual fatherlessness is a problem in the Body of Christ and, although the consequences may be different, it is no less problematic.

In *The Vanguard Leader*, Pastor Frank Damazio writes, "Today, young leaders search desperately for models they can imitate and look up to. When religious systems are corrupt and modern ministry does not offer a mentoring model, young leaders end up following wrong models." (15)

Having good examples to follow and learn from is a critical part of an apostolic leadership culture. Paul's apostolic charge to the Thessalonians to stay in the love of God and the steadfastness of Christ was couched in scriptures such as, "For you yourselves know how you ought to follow our example ... but in order to offer ourselves as a model for you, so that you would follow our example" (2 Thessalonians 3:7–9).

The writer of Hebrews admonishes everyone to follow the faith and conduct of their leaders (Hebrews 13:7). In other words, a person is designed to follow or imitate others before they initiate leadership behaviour. As Daft noted, everyone, including leaders, are followers by nature. (16) The impressionable nature of children or new believers reflects the seriousness of this leadership role. Jesus strongly warned against causing "little ones" who believe in Him to stumble (Luke 17:2). No wonder James said that teachers "incur a stricter judgment" (James 3:1).

When pastors or leaders in the local church neglect the relational nature of the Body of Christ, God's best role models (fathers) are usually in short supply, making spiritual fatherlessness unavoidable. There may be great teaching, diverse ministry events and effective organisational structures, but the more personal touch is absent, at times. This is similar to a father whose successful career makes him a good financial provider, but who is personally detached and uninvolved in the development of his children. The subsequent rejection and insecurity is the source of a range of social ills. Similarly, when spiritual fathers are missing, the Church becomes plagued with problems.

> **When spiritual fathers are missing, the Church becomes plagued with problems.**

One such problem is the difficulty experienced by twentysomethings to find their place in the Church. Research by the Barna Group revealed that people in their twenties and thirties were more likely than older adults to think of themselves as leaders, and that mentoring was the most appealing form of leadership development for young adults. Yet, only four per cent of young adults are currently involved in any form of leadership in the Church. The reason for this low percentage is that mentoring or fathering of new leaders is falling short of demand.

According to Barna, the twentysomethings are "crystallising their views of life without the input of church leaders or other mature Christians". (17) This does not bode well for sustainable transformation. Addressing fatherlessness in the Church, Randall Kittle asks, "Where are the fathers in God's House? We have plenty of pastors and teachers, but where are true spiritual fathers?" (18)

Kittle says that the re-emerging apostolic ministry will heal the wounds of fatherlessness in the Church. He said, "God has been moving in the Church across the face of the earth declaring the love of the Father, and releasing a fresh wave of apostolic ministry to heal the wound of fatherlessness." (19) Kittle's position on familial relationships and fathering reflects the Apostle Paul's approach to church life and leadership development. The quantity and quality of familial rhetoric in Paul's letters reveal how deep the correlation between the family and the Church is.

For Paul, the metaphorical use of familial terms was a common literary tool. It reflected his Hebrew cultural roots. The customs of Jewish families were distinctly different from Greco-Roman culture. Alfred Eldersheim, an Anglican Bible scholar writing on the Jewish traditions and the life of Christ, noted

For Paul, there was only one relationship best suited for leadership development, namely parenting.

that the grand distinction which divided mankind into Jews and Gentiles was not only religious, but familial. (20)

He said, "However frequent and close the intercourse between the two parties, above all, the family life, stood in marked contrast to what would be seen elsewhere. When we consider the relations between man and wife, children and parents, the young and the aged, the vast difference between Judaism and heathenism is so striking." (21) So stark was this contrast that the Roman historian, Tacitus, noted that only the Jews and the ancient Germans considered killing their children a crime. A Roman father's rejection of his child at birth could lead to the killing of the child by suffocation, starvation or exposure.

Equally noteworthy is that Paul did not emphasise the role of rabbi in his mentoring relationship with Timothy. This was despite the fact that by the time of Paul, the function of the rabbi had usurped the father's primary teaching role, in compliance with a rabbinical interpretation of the command in Deuteronomy 17:11 not to disregard the verdict and teaching of the priest in a dispute between parties.

For Paul, there was only one relationship best suited for leadership development, namely parenting. His prolific use of parenting rhetoric supports this assertion. In *Paul's Metaphors*, David Williams noted that Paul continually used parental and child images to emphasise the degree of mutual affection and responsibility needed in leadership. (22) By placing himself in a parent/child framework with young leaders like Timothy and Titus, Paul set the stage for a leadership development model characterised by deep affection, sacrifice, honour and empowerment.

While addressing the issue of family in the 21st century, Dr Broocks said, "The character of the Church is supposed to reflect the character of the family." (23) Paul's directive to Timothy to treat older men as fathers, younger men as brothers, older women as mothers and younger women as sisters (I Timothy 5:1–2) supports this assertion that the family is the relational benchmark of the Church.

According to Scripture, the familial role of a father is a function of apostolic ministry. Paul highlighted this point as validation of his own apostolic leadership when he wrote, "For though you might have ten thousand instructors in Christ, yet you do not have many fathers ... for you are the seal of my apostleship." The strong familial language used by Paul, for example "To Timothy my beloved son" and "To Titus, my true child in a common faith", reflects the prominence of his familial role.

Under the loving tutelage of Paul, both Titus and Timothy emerged as leaders of significant scope. The story of Paul's love and how it transformed Timothy is a classic study in the significance of spiritual fathering. The fact that Paul could leave Titus in Crete to appoint elders and Timothy in Ephesus to take over his leadership role, reflects the effectiveness of his familial approach to leadership development.

Dr Winston highlights this love-based approach to leadership from the Beatitude, "Blessed are those who mourn." (24) According to Augsburger, "to mourn is to deeply care". It denotes a depth of love capable of redeeming someone from aberrant and destructive behaviour. This immense love is the ideal environment

Apostles are first and foremost fathers.

for developing character and releasing destiny. Contrasting fear-based motivation with love-based motivation, Richard Daft says that leading with fear "creates avoidance behaviour", which inhibits growth and change. He says it weakens trust and communication. However, love-based leadership, which is the nature of a father, "builds trust, creativity and enthusiasm". (26)

In an article addressing the issue of apostolic teams, veteran pastor and apostolic leader Bill Johnson said, "Apostles are first and foremost fathers. True fathers will incessantly make decisions for the welfare of their children with no thought to personal sacrifice. It is normal for a father to desire his children to surpass him in every way and labour towards that end." (27)

Apostles father by facilitating growth and development in individual Christians and the community of believers. Paul captured the depth of this fathering role when he wrote:

"But we proved to be gentle among you, as a nursing mother tenderly cares for her own children. Having so fond an affection for you, we were well-pleased to impart to you not only the gospel of God but also our own lives, because you had become very dear to us. For you recall, brethren, our labour and hardship, how working night and day so as not to be a burden to any of you ... You are witnesses, and so is God, how devoutly and uprightly and blamelessly we behaved toward you believers ... we were exhorting and encouraging and imploring each one of you as a father would his own children, so that you would walk in a manner worthy of the God who calls you into His own kingdom and glory" (1 Thessalonians 2:7–12).

Interestingly, in this address to the Thessalonians, Paul referred to himself as both a nursing mother tenderly caring for her children and a father who exhorts, encourages and implores his own children. Both paternal and maternal imagery is used by Paul to convey his familial approach to development for an entire community.

Firstly, in Jewish tradition, fathers were the primary educators of children. Although mothers would often share the role, they never eclipsed the father's primary focus. In *The Jewish Father: Past and Present*, Chaim Waxman noted that fathers played the central role in their son's occupational training and, if they neglected the task, they were accused of teaching their sons to steal. To not prepare a son for his vocation was a father's shame, while developing a son for a trade was deemed a father's crown. (28)

Secondly, Waxman highlighted the mother as the primary provider of affection. He said, "The stereotype of the Jewish mother, familiar in many lands, has firm roots in the Jewish community. No matter what you do, no matter what happens, she will love you always. She may have odd and sometimes irritating ways of showing it, but in a hazardous and unstable world, the belief about the mother's love is strong and unshakable." (29)

While addressing the role of motherhood in Paul's letters, William Ramsey noted, "In the woman's nature, the maternal instinct presented itself as a force that had more absolute power over her than any emotion in a man's nature over him." (30) It represents an inexhaustible supply of motivation and sensitivity in the relationship.

Paul's parental language was both motherly (deeply nurturing) and fatherly (strategically directive). Herein lies the familial complement between intrinsic affection and acceptance, which is independent from performance, and extrinsic growth indicators like learning, change and responsibility. It is evident that the Pauline model for leadership development was loaded

> **Paul's parental language was both motherly (deeply nurturing) and fatherly (strategically directive).**

with unconditional love, purposeful strategies, improvement and promotion. Finally, Paul's language to the Thessalonians was for all believers and not just for Timothy and Titus. It was consistent with the clan-based system of first-century Mediterranean society.

Vernon Robbins notes that, among members of a family, all goods and services were freely given. (31) Rather than being reserved for a select few, this familial model became part of the church culture. Cannistraci contends that, because the same qualities essential to families are needed in the family of God, a new generation of spiritual fathers will be enlisted by the Holy Spirit. (32) He sees them bringing their stability and strength not only to a movement, but to the entire Body of Christ. (33) Although there seems to be a general dearth of spiritual fathering in the Church today, a restoration promised through the prophet Malachi seems imminent.

"Behold, I am going to send you Elijah the prophet before the coming of the great and terrible day of the Lord. He will restore the hearts of the fathers to their children and the hearts of the children to their fathers, so that I will not come and smite the land with a curse" (Malachi 4:5–6).

According to the Biblical pattern, apostles are fathers who provide love, discipline, provision, reproduction and blessing to individual believers and churches. From recent trends in South Africa, we see Christian leaders and their organisations acting more paternally towards the next generation of spiritual sons and daughters. Rhema, His People, Doxa Deo and Shofar expend a lion's share of their time, energy and resources reaching and developing high school and university students.

Leaders like Michael Cassidy and his organisation African Enterprise are focusing more on leadership development of South Africa's younger generation. Having the heart of a father, coupled with a heavenly mandate and anointing, enables apostolic leaders like Michael Cassidy to foster a culture conducive to leadership development and social transformation. This leadership development culture is realised through cultivating multigenerational relationships.

The Power of Multigenerational Living

Although not explicitly stated, the language used in the Book of Acts, I Corinthians and 1 and 2 Timothy implies that Timothy was converted through Paul's ministry during his first missionary journey. The transpiring events at Lystra, Timothy's home town, indicate that Timothy's first encounters with Paul took place at a time of intense persecution, deep personal sacrifice and prolific leadership deployment. We see that the relationship between Paul and Timothy began in the classroom of real-life issues, personal vulnerability and focused action. Therefore, the relational requirements for working with Paul in the long term came as no surprise to Timothy. Equally significant is that, in 2 Timothy 1:5, Paul recognises the sincerity of Timothy's faith as first being evident in his grandmother Lois, and then in his mother Eunice.

The fact that Paul frames Timothy's faith in generational language is noteworthy. Timothy's sincere faith, which Paul referred to as one of the goals of his instruction and mentoring, is seamlessly passed on from one generation to the next. The Psalmist captured the value that God places on labouring among and between the various generations when he wrote,

> **Seamless multigenerational partnerships are by divine design.**

"Your faithfulness continues throughout all generations" (Psalm 119:90). Seamless multigenerational partnerships are by divine design.

69

The notion of progress stemming from the passage of value from one generation to the next is part of Jewish cultural tradition. Rela M. Geffen, President of Baltimore Hebrew University, noted that the celebration and renewal rites for birth, marriage and death reflect Judaism's positive perspective on the unending circle of life: from conception through death and back again to life through the continuity of the generations. These rituals, having communal orientation, link Jews across space and time, tying their personal history with that of the Jewish people. (34)

So fundamental was this multigenerational value that God made it commandment number five in the Decalogue: "Honour your father and your mother, that your days may be prolonged in the land which the Lord your God gives you" (Exodus 20:12). As a Hebrew and a Pharisee, Paul was well acquainted with customs regarding the training of children, the giving of inheritance and the transfer of privilege and responsibility.

In the book of Deuteronomy, there are more than 40 accounts of Moses instructing people to train children. Cross-generational relationships were the primary conduit for value exchange. From scriptures such as "A good man leaves an inheritance to his children's children" (Proverbs 13:22); "Even when I am old and grey, O God, do not forsake me, until I declare Your strength to this generation" (Psalm 71:18); and "We will not conceal them from their children, but tell to the generation to come" (Psalm 78:4), we see the strategy emerging of an experienced generation serving a younger generation for the purpose of future progress.

The quality of leadership development is proportional to the manner and degree of one generation's connection and contribution to the next.

Addressing seven strategic shifts to successfully navigate the 21st century, Mark Conner wrote, "Each generation is responsible to pass the baton of God's purposes on to the next generation. God requires us to leave a heritage and inheritance for those who follow after us." (35) The quality of leadership development is proportional to the manner and degree of one generation's connection and contribution to the next.

70

The psalmist states unequivocally that God's plans for humanity are revealed from "generation to generation" (Psalm 33:11). Conner calls it having a "generation perspective." (36) To borrow a term from one of the most modern trends in housing: developing and releasing leaders is best realised through "multigenerational living." (37)

The priority of a multigenerational alliance advancing the Kingdom is highlighted by Timothy's natural and spiritual family. Interestingly, Paul uses language to emphasise generations beyond just himself and Timothy (parent and child). Once again, Paul's knowledge of Jewish history and practice informs his exhortation. He was keenly aware of how well Joshua had succeeded Moses in leading Israel. Moses proved to be a good mentor to Joshua, but Joshua neglected to mentor his own successor. Conner noted, "He failed to pass the baton on to the next generation. He did not train a successor." (38)

After Joshua, another generation arose that did not know God or his purposes (Judges 2:10). If the ceiling of one generation is meant to be the floor of the next generation, then the exchange between major age groups is of paramount importance. Is it any wonder that God introduced Himself as the God of Abraham, Isaac and Jacob? We see Him building through and across generations.

A New Testament version of the complementary nature of three generations is found in 1 John 2:12–13. John writes, "I am writing to you, little children … fathers … young men." The faith of a child, the fight of a young man and the foresight, insight and hindsight of a father inform the process of growth and productivity. Put differently, the confidence of a child, the courage of a young man and the character of a father are reciprocating and reinforcing qualities in multigenerational living.

Labouring with three generations in mind represents both the receiving and the giving aspects of learning and leadership. Not only do leaders require mature and experienced input for success, but they also need a successor to further the process of improvement. Progress is defined as advancing or moving forward in space, time, knowledge, character or

> **Labouring with three generations in mind represents both the receiving and the giving aspects of learning and leadership.**

matter. (39) One generation benefiting from the successes and failures of a previous generation is basic to most productivity and progress. Of course, the advantages of multigenerational relationships are experienced mutually.

The benefit exchange between different age groups is not nearly as one-sided as some tend to view it. An apostolic leadership culture is where young and old can be celebrated and activated in fruitful collaboration. There is little doubt that the strength, energy and passion of youth requires the wisdom, guidance and tempering of maturity and experience to avoid becoming prodigal, but equally true, the tempered and experienced elder requires robust engagement with the younger generation to avoid becoming rigid, sedentary and regressive.

Moses and Joshua represent two generations that complemented each other for a greater purpose. Firstly, Joshua, the younger protégé of Moses, was entrusted with leading a nation into the Promised Land. The commission given to Joshua was not just because of his youthful strength and unique skills, but also because of a rich investment by Moses. Secondly, Scripture emphasises Moses' physical prowess. Although he was 120 years old, "his eye was not dim, nor his vigour abated (Deuteronomy 34:7). This was due, at least in part, to his continued service in mentoring the next generation.

An apostolic leadership culture is where young and old can be celebrated and activated in fruitful collaboration.

Studies done on ageing have found support for the premise that the older generation benefits enormously from activities that are physically and relationally demanding. The Harvard Study of Adult Development, the most comprehensive study on ageing ever conducted, notes that regular exercise and close personal relationships are critical to healthy ageing.

Dr George Vaillant, Director of this Harvard study, and senior physician at Brigham and Women's Hospital in Boston, noted that curiosity and creativity helped transform older people into seemingly younger ones. "Individuals who are always learning something new about the world, maintaining a playful spirit, and finding younger friends as they lose older ones are making the most of the ageing process." (40)

When the older generation walks with the younger generation, it reaps life-force benefits. The younger generation gains knowledge and understanding, while the older generation reaps joy and fulfilment. As Paul said to Timothy, "Longing to see you ... that I may be filled with joy" (2 Timothy 1:4).

One of the purest examples of how this works comes from an old movie, Heidi. Heidi was a young orphan girl who had been sent to live with her grandfather after the death of her parents. She had never met her grandfather because he was a recluse living in the mountains.

The first encounter between Heidi and her grandfather is little more than a vivacious bundle of curiosity meeting Stonehenge. When Heidi first moves into the mountain cabin, her grandfather is completely detached and stoic. Yet, an amazing metamorphosis takes place. As he serves Heidi's basic needs (food and lodging), he comes to life emotionally. By the end of the movie, Heidi's grandfather is a new man, full of joy, purpose and passion. There are certain life benefits that can only be gained in reciprocal multigenerational relationships.

When the older and younger generations become polarised, we get *Lord of the Flies* on the one hand, and *Grumpy Old Men* on the other. In Lord of the Flies, we have young schoolboys who are shipwrecked on a desert island. Lacking any parental input, they descend into barbarism. In *Grumpy Old Men*, two old friends, identifying with no one but themselves, regress into the worst kind of adolescent behaviour.

If there were any truth to the so-called "generation gap theory, some unbridgeable chasm between young and old, then we would all be in serious trouble because God is called the "Ancient of Days". God is not relatable and relevant to us because He is just like us, but because He possesses what we need. Different age groups are important to one another simply because each generation has something the others need.

> **God is not relatable and relevant to us because He is just like us, but because He possesses what we need.**

Wise and experienced military leaders need the physical strength and fortitude of young soldiers to win battles. Parents and teachers need a child's curiosity and passion to pass on a legacy. God has designed certain features in every age group to be an inspiration to the others. The laughter of a child, the courage of a young man and the maturity of an elder are meant to leaven all of life. Going into the promised land of Kingdom living requires a new level of generational partnerships. When God called Moses to lead Israel out of Egypt, part of Pharaoh's opposition related to this multigenerational influence. In Exodus 10:8, Pharaoh finally relented and said to Moses, "Go, serve the Lord your God." He then asked, "Who are the ones that are going?" Moses told Pharaoh that they would be taking the young and the old with them. Although Pharaoh was prepared to release Moses and the young men, he was not about to let the children and the elderly go. Why? Because He knew that Moses could not leave Egypt without them.

Once Pharaoh heard Moses' intention to take the children and the elderly, he accused Moses of having an evil intent. In other words, he knew Israel intended leaving Egypt for good. When all three generations work well together, historical restraints are left behind for a better tomorrow. The Promised Land of bringing the Kingdom "on earth as it is in heaven" is realised through the quality of generational synergy.

At Rephidim, Israel was confronted by Amalek (Exodus 17). After Moses had sent Joshua and his soldiers out to do battle, he positioned himself on a hill overlooking the battlefield. As long as the young men could see his hand and staff raised, they prevailed in the battle, but as Moses' hands grew tired and were lowered, they started losing.

So, Aaron and Hur sat Moses on a rock and held his arms up until the battle was won. This story provides a good picture of what happens when mutual honour and respect is bestowed in multigenerational partnerships. As the parent generation extend the hand and staff of honour, guidance and authority, the younger generation are positioned and empowered to prevail over their enemies. Of course, the older generation reap the benefit of support and renewed strength. According to the Pauline model, these familial relationships are meant to produce multigenerational partnerships, where progress and succession are constant. He explicitly charged Timothy to take what he had seen and heard from him and pass it on to others, who would then pass it on to others (2 Timothy 2:2).

Implicit in Paul's directive is the progressive advancement of the Kingdom. The fact that these men had "upset the world" (Acts 17:6) during the lifetime of Paul's ministry reflects the expansive and transformational nature of this relational model. Of course, the best evidence of multigenerational success is a 2 000-year history, where a renegade Jewish sect went from being locally persecuted to globally triumphant.

It helps with answering the question asked by Albert Laszlo Barabasi in his

The transformational impact of one generation loving and serving another generation is a ubiquitous feature in human history.

book, Linked, "How did the unorthodox beliefs of a small and disdained Jewish sect come to form the basis of the Western world's dominant religion?" (41) The transformational impact of one generation loving and serving another generation is a ubiquitous feature in human history.

Among the contemporary leaders most effective at modelling this relational and generational approach is Nelson Mandela. Known affectionately as the father (Madiba) of the new South Africa, he epitomises this love-based leadership. As Mamphela Ramphele noted, "Mandela does what he does out of a deep love for his people." (42) His commitment to partnering with the next generation is noteworthy.

On Youth Day in 1995, Mandela said, "On behalf of the government, I wish to say once more that no one receives the attention of our government like the youth." (43) At the inauguration ceremony of the University of the Witwatersrand's new Vice-Chancellor, he spoke of merging the knowledge and achievements of previous generations with the exploration, creativity and adaptability of the new. He called it the "crucial intersection of tradition and renewal." (43) Certainly, the South African miracle can be credited, to a large extent, to this magnanimous and fatherly leadership approach.

Within this macrocosm of South African transformation are numerous examples of two, three and even four generations of leaders benefiting from the sacrifices and investments of those who went before them. In particular, there is the labour of Nigel and Debbie Desmond at His People Church in Grahamstown, in the Eastern Cape, South Africa, which reflects the Pauline model of familial relationships and generational partnerships.

After graduating from the University of Cape Town in 1991, and with a good investment from their spiritual father, Pastor Paul Daniel (first generation), they were sent out to pioneer a campus church at Rhodes University in Grahamstown.

Eventually, the ministry became so successful that hundreds of students were reached, trained and released throughout the nation.

Nigel and Debbie (second generation) trained up a strong couple, Gareth and Taryn Lowe (third generation), who were now able to lead the church; releasing them to pioneer a new work in the city of East London. The strength of this generational exchange continued as Gareth and Taryn, who are now pioneering in Germany, were able to hand the Grahamstown church over to the leadership of Tendai and Keryn Chitsike (fourth generation).

The continued health and strength of His People Church in Grahamstown is due, at least in part, to this seamless exchange between various generations of leaders. It is interesting to note that from the leadership of this Grahamstown church has flowed numerous training materials on nation-building in South Africa. Nation-building is a long-term enterprise requiring multiple seasons of change, innovation and hard work passing from one generation to the next.

Conclusion

When Jesus said, "If you love Me, you will keep My commandments" (John 14:15, italics added), He was advocating what many leaders can sometimes lose sight of: the nature of the relationship determining the quality of the decision. Love-based relationship is fundamental to a Pauline/apostolic model of leadership development.

In his thought-provoking book, Connecting, Larry Crabb nailed his relational colours to the mast when he wrote, "Connecting is more central than obedience." (45) Relationships, and more specifically, familial relationships, are basic to the kind of interaction conducive to developing an apostolic leadership culture.

Connecting is more central than obedience.

Among the familial roles most catalytic for generating this Kingdom culture is spiritual fathering. It creates multigenerational partnerships capable of effective and sustainable transformation. In The New Mystics, a comprehensive look at the history of revival, John Crowder calls reproduction the "chief focus of the apostolic". (46) He calls apostles "fathers", whose success is measured in the passing of the baton to another generation, which then exceed previous levels of ministry and gifting.

He writes, "The children must reach further than the fathers. They must go further — build higher — on the foundations we have laid." In Chapter Four, we look at another critical partnership for bringing in the Kingdom of God: mission-directed team leadership.

Discussion Questions

3.1 On a scale from 1–10, how significant are relationships in your current ministry or work environment; how would you describe the nature of these relationships; and would those you work with agree?

3.2 What is so important about familial relationships in building a Kingdom culture?

3.3 Give several examples from Scripture of effective multigenerational relationships. How do these apply to your life?

3.4 How would you describe and implement fathering in your ministry or work environment?

3.5 Do you currently have examples in your relational environment that reflect healthy multigenerational partnerships? If so, what would an improved state look like; if not, what needs to change?

CHAPTER FOUR

Mission-directed Team Leadership

I n *The 21 Irrefutable Laws of Leadership*, John Maxwell echoed the importance of team leadership when he said, "At forty, I realised that my success wasn't going to be determined by my gifts, my talents, or my opportunities, but by my ability to develop a great team." (1) This realisation led to him identifying the "Law of the Inner Circle" (those closest to you determine your level of success), making the development of a team his number one priority. (2)

The notion that the output and impact of two is greater than that of one is not a novel idea. Its origin is as old as creation. When God said, "It is not good for the man to be alone" (Genesis 2:18, italics added), He confirmed the priority of productivity through relationships and/ or teams. The Hebrew word for good is

> **The notion that the output and impact of two is greater than that of one is not a novel idea.**

towb, and in Genesis 2 it is used to mean useful and profitable.

Interestingly, when Jethro, Moses' father-in-law, saw Moses judging all the people by himself, he said, "The thing that you are doing is not good" (Exodus 18:17, italics added). In other words, this will not be profitable for you or the people. Moses heeded Jethro's advice by developing a team of judges from Israel's various tribes (ibid. v. 25), which resulted in all the people going "to their place in peace" (ibid. v. 23, italics added). The word, peace, shalom (Hebrew) and eirene (Greek), is a comprehensive word denoting health, welfare, prosperity and all things good. According to Paul, peace is the nature of the Kingdom (Romans 14:17) and team leadership is its key facilitator (Ephesians 4:11).

In his thought-provoking book, *Culture of Honor*, Danny Silk calls peace "the primary quality of the government of God". (3) An apostolic approach to team leadership is based on the notion that a synergy of diverse leadership roles and functions is critical for maturing a community of believers and advancing the Kingdom of peace.

The apostle Paul emphasised the scale and scope of team leadership when he wrote, "He gave some as apostles, and some as prophets, and some as evangelists, and some as pastors and teachers, for the equipping of the saints for the work of service ... until we all attain ... to the measure of the stature which belongs to the fullness of Christ" (Ephesians 4:11– 13).

His references to the role of foundational ministries (apostles and prophets), local church governance (elders and deacons) and congregational ministries (prophecy, service, teaching, exhortation, giving and mercy) highlight the necessity of team leadership and ministry. One of the most prolific features of an apostolic leadership culture is that diverse personalities, callings, gifts, skills and ministries complement each other within a team, around the common mission of advancing this Kingdom of peace.

What does an effective mission-directed team look like? Why is it so significant and what are some of its vital contributions for effecting sustainable transformation? Team effectiveness can be defined as accomplishing performance goals within a collaborative environment of common purpose, complementary skills and mutual accountability. (4) Richard Daft called mission and goal incompatibility the single greatest cause of team conflict. (5) In *The Wisdom of Teams*, Jon Katzenbach and Douglas Smith assert that, if a team fails to establish performance goals, or if those goals do not relate to the team's overall mission, team members become confused, pull apart and revert to mediocre performance. (6)

For an individual apostle and for the apostolic leadership culture, the mission and goal is larger than any single strategy, ministry thrust or local church focus.

In his 1991 New Year's message to the people of South Africa, Nelson Mandela highlighted how the success of Codesa (Congress for the Democratisation of

South Africa) was tied to one common objective: attaining a non-racial democracy. (7) Although the strength of Codesa came from the diversity of "political parties and persuasion", it was the common purpose of having "one South Africa, one nation, one vote and one future" that directed its success.

For an individual apostle and for the apostolic leadership culture, the mission and goal is larger than any single strategy, ministry thrust or local church focus. As argued in Chapter One, the purpose and goal of apostolic ministry is to successfully reach and establish people, their communities and their cities in Kingdom truth and order. The Kingdom of God coming "on earth as it is in heaven" was the message, mission and mandate given to the apostles and, although the local church is a primary vehicle for bringing the Kingdom, the Kingdom's reach and influence extends beyond any local church or movement of churches.

The successful rebuilding of the walls of Jerusalem under Nehemiah's leadership underscores this point. It reveals the scale and scope of effective mission-directed team leadership.

Nehemiah's Mission-directed Leadership Team

Nehemiah (an Old Testament apostolic leader) and his apostolic team (priests, nobles, officials and the rest of the Jews) acted effectively, from mission to strategy to structure to process. Nehemiah and his team first committed to the mission and overall strategy (Nehemiah 2:17–18), and then created a relevant structure and process for repairing and building the gates and walls (Nehemiah 3).

Even when faced with new environmental threats (Sanballat, Tobiah and Geshom), there was a timely exchange of new ideas, energy and action, which translated into new structures (family-based labour), flexible processes (working with one hand and fighting with the other) and improved warning systems (the trumpet blast). Buy-in to the broader mission/goal was critical to their team's effective action and subsequent success. In most leadership teams and partnerships, this mission-directed approach can help leaders and their communities avoid the pitfalls of parochialism and personal agendas.

The ability of South Africans to bring transformation to cities, a feat accomplished by early Christians, will depend on ideas and actions breaching the boundaries of insular organisational loyalties. It will require an attitude and approach echoed by Nelson Mandela when he called for "artists, musicians, sportspersons, religious leaders, traditional institutions, intellectuals, media and all who give leadership" to join hands in the common goal of building the moral fibre of the nation. (8)

Author and apostolic leader Floyd McClung calls it "a new kind of Christianity ... one that captures the hearts and minds of those outside the church walls". (9) He says, "The apostolic calling of the followers of Jesus includes forging new ways for how we do church and pioneering new places where we do church." (10)

Nehemiah's apostolic model highlighted some essential features of effective team leadership and ministry. Among them are:

1. Initiated by God
While this would seem to be a no-brainer, considering Gamaliel's advice, "If it is of God, you will not be able to overthrow them" (Acts 5:39) and Paul's admonition, "But we will not boast beyond our measure, but within the measure of the sphere which God apportioned to us as a measure" (2 Corinthian 10:13), there are many works initiated by human effort alone. Paul says "they measure themselves by themselves and compare themselves with themselves" (2 Corinthian 10:12).

When describing his initial intercession for Jerusalem, and his subsequent favour with King Artaxerxes and the Jewish leaders, Nehemiah used rhetoric that was clearly doxological, i.e. his efforts were inspired and directed by, from and for God. The connection between God impetus and teaming up to rebuild the city is also evident in Nehemiah's response to some early opposition. He said, "The God of heaven will give us success" (Nehemiah 2:20, italics added). When the job was finished in just 52 days, Nehemiah said their enemies had lost confidence because they recognised that the work had been accomplished with the help of God (Nehemiah 6:16).

Of course, Jesus set the standard for any God-initiated ministry when He said, "The Son can do nothing of Himself, unless it is something He sees the Father doing" (John 5:19). Paul and Barnabas's partnership and first missionary journey were initiated by a word from the Holy Spirit. Luke writes, "While they were ministering to the Lord and fasting, the Holy Spirit said, 'Set apart for Me Barnabas and Saul for the work to which I have called them'" (Acts 13:2). That God-initiated work provided Barnabas and Saul with another important team quality, common purpose.

2. A common purpose

Once Nehemiah had finished describing God's favourable hand upon him, the people said, "Let us arise and build" (Nehemiah 2:18). The greater purpose of rebuilding the walls and gates was critical to generating team cohesiveness and impact. Daft defines team cohesiveness as the extent to which team members remain united in pursuit of a common goal. (11) He says, "When team members agree on a purpose, they are more cohesive." (12) This quality rings true throughout Nehemiah's leadership tenure. When threatened with attack, Nehemiah's pep talk consisted of, "Remember the Lord who is great and awesome, and fight for your brothers, your sons, your daughters, your wives and your houses" (Nehemiah 4:14).

Although Nehemiah's rhetoric seems directed towards the self-interest of individual families, this familial language was descriptive of the whole community, various generations and their inheritance. This was a God-centred, community-grounded and future-focused reminder, which fostered kingdom unity and decisive action. Commenting on the strength and impact of the civil rights movement under the leadership of Martin Luther King Jr., Donald Phillips noted, "Martin worked with his team to set lofty, sweeping goals for the movement around which people could unite." (13) He went on to say, "Having such a specific purpose served to facilitate action and decisiveness." (14) Of course, as history records, Martin Luther King's communication skills were an essential part of energising people around a common purpose.

> **This was a God-centred, community-grounded and future-focused reminder, which fostered kingdom unity and decisive action.**

3. Good communication

From Nehemiah's early dialogue with the king and the Jewish leaders, to his ongoing exhortations and encouragement, to the use of trumpets for rallying the people, the application of effective communication was essential to their success. Communication is defined as "a process by which information and understanding is transferred between a sender and a receiver". (15) Good communication is a necessary skill or tool that can inspire and unite people around a purpose or mission. It was said of Martin Luther King Jr. that his ability to communicate created a purpose and identity that had not existed before. (16)

Similarly, Jesus and his early apostles rallied countless individuals, relationships and churches around the new purpose of bringing the Kingdom into all walks of life. Their ability to communicate effectively was a primary catalyst. As the writer of Proverbs noted, "The tongue of the wise makes knowledge acceptable ... a soothing tongue is a tree of life ... the lips of the wise spread knowledge ... and how delightful is a timely word!" (Proverbs 15:2–23).

Weighing in on the role of communication in team effectiveness, Katzenbach and Smith state, "Common understanding and purpose cannot arise without effective communication and constructive conflict that, in turn, depend on interpersonal skills." (17) Put another way, effective communication creates an environment of understanding where a diversity of leaders can work together in complementary relationships.

4. A continuous supply of diverse and complementary   leaders

In his book, *The 17 Indisputable laws of Teamwork*, John Maxwell highlights the approach to organisational achievement advocated by Vince Lombardi, a National Football League champion coach. Lombardi said, "The achievements of an organisation are the results of the combined efforts of every individual." (18)

The volume and type of leaders and people involved in Jerusalem's restoration process is quite staggering. Members of this prolific team were priests, Levites, city officials, gatekeepers, guards, farmers, jewellers, pharmacists, merchants, temple servants and even perfumers. Even more amazing was the degree of co-operation and coordination. (19)

All throughout the account, we find the phrase "next to him" worked so and so, and "next to them" worked others. Each one was assigned a section of the wall or a specific gate. Although these large numbers would be impractical for most mission-directed teams today, they do highlight another fundamental quality of an apostolic team culture: for everyone an opportunity, and everyone a potential leader. (20)

Paul's every member approach to team leadership is evident in almost every letter he wrote. For example, Paul told the Romans, "To all who are beloved of God in Rome ... God has allotted to each a measure of faith" (Romans 1:7 and Romans 12:3). He reminded the Corinthians, "But to each one is given the manifestation of the Spirit for the

> **For everyone an opportunity, and everyone a potential leader.**

common good" (1 Corinthians 12:7) and, to the Galatians, he said, "Therefore you are no longer a slave, but a son; and if a son, then an heir through God" (Galatians 4:7).

With the exception of a few leaders like Timothy and Titus, Paul addressed his letters to "all the saints" at Ephesus, Philippi, Colossae and Thessalonica, thereby signifying that every believer had been commissioned by God to bring the Kingdom. In *Culture of Honor,* Danny Silk connects a successful team design to the function of honour within a community of people. He says, "Diverse anointings each contribute something entirely unique to the project of bringing heaven to earth, and this requires an honouring (and undemocratic) attitude that says, 'You have something I don't have, and I need what you have.'" (21)

In *Go Teams*, Blanchard, Randolph and Grazier call having diverse talents, skills, values and personalities the strength of any team. (22) The same honour found within a leadership team can be extended to the whole Body when each and every person understands their significance and is free to do their part in bringing the Kingdom. This creates a perpetual pool of leaders that supplies the development of new teams.

Emerging from this honour-filled leadership culture is another valuable asset for mission-directed teams, namely the currency of trust.

5. The currency of trust

How many of us have ignored our petrol gauge's low-warning light to the point of embarrassment? We are suddenly stranded in frenetic traffic in our brilliantly engineered automobile, which is now about as welcomed as a terrorist leading children's church. When the fuel is gone, that amazing wonder of technology, our car, is rather useless. Similarly, when the fuel of trust drains out, we lose the ability to do real teamwork.

Addressing contemporary leadership issues, Tom Peters calls trust the "issue of the decade". He places its importance above any technology or system. In *The Five Dysfunctions of Team*, Patrick Lencioni calls trust the heart of a "functioning, cohesive team". (23) Most leaders would agree that trust is the most catalytic ingredient in a team's chemistry. Daft cites a survey of senior leaders who considered building trust the most important and most difficult leadership task related to successful teams. (24)

> **When the fuel of trust drains out, we lose the ability to do real teamwork.**

In his book *The Speed of Trust* Stephan Covey argues that character, competence and track record are all critical elements in fostering trust. The high level of trust afforded to Nehemiah by the Jews living in and around Jerusalem is noteworthy. His relationship with God, his favour with the king and his ability to assess and plan for the citywide project were indicative of Nehemiah's character and competence.

The fact that so many would follow Nehemiah's leadership, in spite of the life-threatening conditions, reveals enormous trust. That trust is actualised in Nehemiah 2, 3 and 4 through another key aspect of effective team leadership, namely strategy.

6. A well-planned overall strategy

Daft calls strategic leadership one of the most critical issues facing organisations. (25) A team's effectiveness begins to materialise when a broad purpose or mission is translated into specific strategies and measurable goals. Nehemiah spent significant time distilling the citywide mandate into specific goals and actions. Even before he left Susa for Jerusalem, he made plans to acquire the materials needed for the walls, gates and a house (Nehemiah 2:8). He then spent three days assessing the conditions and identifying the building strategy and process (Nehemiah 2:11–15).

The overall strategy was clear: to rebuild the gates, the walls and other structures. Despite the other team functions involved such as common purpose, diverse leaders, communication and trust, it is unlikely the work could have been accomplished without Nehemiah's planning process.

Interestingly, the successful launch of the new South Africa in 1994, with the first fully democratic elections in South African history, was predicated on God-inspired action, a shared purpose and mission, the tireless efforts of a multitude of diverse leaders and people, relentless communication and a ton of trust based on vulnerability. Yet, as significant as these essentials were, they could not have accomplished so much in so little time without the implementation of well-devised plans.

In his State of the Nation address on 6 February 1998, South African President Nelson Mandela attributed their success to "clear strategy, properly managed plans and good governance". (26) Addressing the issue of strategy in South Africa, Gerhard van Rensburg called for strategy and planning that was flexible and treated as a guideline. (27) Just like Nehemiah, leaders and their teams in South Africa should approach strategy, not as fixed and detailed, but as flexible enough to handle the "unexpected changes and challenges" that are common features within the African and global landscapes.

7. Flexibility and adaptability

In *the Leadership Lessons of Jesus*, Bob Briner and Ray Pritchard refer to leadership as a complex undertaking that requires both "steadfast determination and thoughtful flexibility". (28) The opportunities and threats in Jerusalem presented Nehemiah with an environment requiring both determination and flexibility. Rebuilding the walls and gates amid life-threatening conditions required unwavering determination, but being flexible enough to adapt to changing conditions was equally critical.

Jack Walsh, former Chief Executive Officer of General Electric, said the "end is in sight" when changes in the environment exceed changes made by leadership. (29) Nehemiah adjusted his tactics on two occasions: once, when he heard that attacks were imminent, and again, when there was an outcry from the people because of the burden of usury. On both occasions, Nehemiah was able to implement significant adjustments, leading to a safer and well-motivated team progressing towards the common goal.

> **The 'end is in sight' when changes in the environment exceed changes made by leadership.**

87

As highlighted by Jon Katzenbach and Douglas Smith, good team leaders become energised by obstacles, rather than discouraged and stuck. They acquire and put to use "fresh facts, different perspectives and new information". (30) In summary, these seven characteristics provide the clarity, connection, chemistry, confidence and capacity necessary for accomplishing audacious goals. Contrary to popular belief, great accomplishments are not the by-product of those going solo. Even the achievements of outstanding innovators like Thomas Edison and Albert Einstein were predicated on the efforts of others before them and around them. Einstein once remarked, "Many times a day I realise how much my own inner and outer life is built upon the labours of my fellow men, both living and dead." (31) As stated earlier, the notion of partnerships and teams producing great things is as old as creation.

As far back as the Genesis account of creation, and God's first man and woman, we find provocative insights relevant to team effectiveness. The Book of Genesis lays the groundwork and framework for countless Kingdom truths. In *The Layman's Bible Commentary*, Fritsch refers to Genesis as "the starting point of all theology". (32) In *A walk Through the Book of Genesis*, Bob Deffenbaugh calls Genesis our historical point of reference from where "all subsequent revelation proceeds". (33)

To augment the previous section's focus on team leadership, we now look at some team characteristics found in the first few chapters of the Book of Genesis. What can we learn from the earliest recorded partnerships or teams found in Genesis?

A Genesis Model for Team Leadership

There are many things we can learn as we study individual lives, specific events and/or issues. However, to learn for the purpose of understanding, change and transferability, those same people, events and issues should be examined within their relational, cultural, environmental and historical contexts. Daft refers to this as the macro side of leadership. (34) It transcends the individual and focuses on the communities where ideas, values and strategies are lived out. For example, if someone really wants to understand my approach to leading and leadership, they would need the reference point of my American cultural experiences, as well as 25 years of ministry relationships in Africa.

The apostle Paul would often refer to his Hebrew roots, educational upbringing, ministry experiences and other relationships to augment significant points. When challenging the Galatians who were falling back into legalism, he said, "For you have heard of my former manner of life ... I was advancing in Judaism beyond many of my contemporaries ... being more extremely zealous for my ancestral traditions ..." (Galatians 1:13–14). That context, as well as his journey among the Gentiles and his relationships with other leaders, gave the Galatians a better frame of reference for receiving Paul's strong correction.

The Book of Genesis is not just about individuals and events, but also about their relationships and partnerships — how God and people teamed up within their environments to forge a better tomorrow. There are three partnerships within the first three chapters of Genesis that offer insights into effective team leadership. For the purpose of simplicity

> **The Book of Genesis is not just about individuals and events, but also about their relationships and partnerships.**

and identification, I have named them Team God, Team Man and Team God and Man.

1. Team God

In the Book of Genesis, we find a partnership, a team in the very first verse. Genesis 1:1 says, "In the beginning God." The Hebrew word for God in this verse is elohiym. It is the plural of elowah. According to the AMG's *Annotated Strong's Hebrew Dictionary of the Old Testament*, the word elohiym refers to gods in the ordinary sense. This does not mean "gods" when referring to the true God of Israel, but its form does allow for plurality within the Godhead, commonly known as the Trinity. Although there is contention over the exact nature of the word elohiym, Trinitarian thought clearly places the Father, Son and Holy Spirit in the role of Creator. Being a team, the Godhead underscores several relevant points.

Firstly, the origin of a team found in the Godhead reinforces the notion of something being designed and initiated by God. One of the more significant outcomes of this revelation is God confidence. When building within an apostolic leadership culture, the ultimate source of confidence is not perfect people, prodigious resources or flawless execution, but being supported and backed up by the perfect team of the Father, Son and Holy Spirit. This was well illustrated by Cannistraci when he called God the separator, sender, source, supervisor and seal of apostolic ministry. (35)

When Luke described Peter and John's arrest in Acts 4, he noted a connection between how confident they were and their relationship to Jesus. Even a disbelieving Sanhedrin recognised a correlation between "them ...having been with Jesus" (Acts 4:13) and the confident stand they were taking. Paul said that his confidence was "not in fleshly wisdom but in the grace of God" (2 Corinthians 1:12).

Secondly, the fact that God is a team (Father, Son and Holy Spirit) implies that the role of a team is not optional. A team isn't just a practical tool that God uses, it's who He is. It's not just a matter of utility; it's a matter of design. For example, our eyes, ears, nose and mouth are not just functional tools; they are part of who we are. This perspective should have a causal effect on the level of value that people attribute to team leadership.

The ultimate source of confidence is not perfect people, prodigious resources or flawless execution, but being supported and backed up by the perfect team of the Father, Son and Holy Spirit.

Generally speaking, people are more vigilant in the care of their physical bodies than their clothing. Imbibing the true value or significance of something is a prime motivator. As we discovered in Chapter Two, what and how we value something or someone is a driving force behind our attitudes, behaviour and actions.

Thirdly, a team has one overall purpose: productivity. As we examine the language of Genesis 1, we find the Godhead creating, producing and improving. Then we hear God's primary command to Adam and Eve, "Be fruitful and multiply, and fill the earth ..." (Genesis 1:28). Solomon, called the wisest man who ever lived, said, "Two are better than one because they have a good return for their labour" (Ecclesiastes 4:9).

All around us, we are reminded of the productive nature of teaming. In mathematics, 1 + 1 = 2; in technology, software + hardware + electricity = worldwide web; in relationships, father + mother = Nelson Mandela; in athletics, strength + speed + stamina + suppleness + skill + strategy = Iron Man champion; and in Christian ministry, word + prayer + anointing + action = changed community. When the apostle John wrote, "Beloved, I pray that in all respects you may prosper and be in good health, just as your soul prospers" (3 John 1:2), he underscored the Father's primary agenda for everyone: to advance or gain in everything.

Paul captured God's productive purpose for humanity when he told the church in Rome that "God causes all things to work together for good" (Romans 8:28, italics added). The Greek word for good is agathos, and it means good in any sense.

Fourthly, according to the language of Genesis 1, a team's greatest asset is good communication. In 28 verses, we find the phrase, "God said", nine different times. The communication is clear and specific, with corresponding action and change. Adding to our previous emphasis on communication, Noah Webster defined communication as, "the act of imparting, conferring or delivering, from one to another; as the communication of

> **A team isn't just a practical tool that God uses, it's who He is.**

knowledge, opinion or facts". To communicate is "to impart; to give to another, as a partaker; to confer for joint possession; to bestow as that which the receiver is to hold, retain, use or enjoy". (36)

Daft calls communication "a process by which information and understanding is transferred between a sender and a receiver". (37) Communication is an exchange of understanding from one person to another for the purpose of intrinsic or extrinsic experience. The priority of good communication cannot be overstated. In *Crucial Conversation*, Parkinson says that any vacuum created by a lack of communication will soon be filled with "poison, drivel and misrepresentation". (38) In other words, ambiguity is the playground of demons.

Interestingly, a communication breakdown was utilised by God to thwart an evil agenda. By simply confusing their language, God was able to stop all work on the Tower of Babel and scatter the people (Genesis 11:7-8). Employing good communication skills is fundamental to any effective partnership or development

> **Any vacuum created by a lack of communication will soon be filled with 'poison, drivel and misrepresentation'.**

process. To successfully embrace the vision of an "African Renaissance", Gerhard Van Rensburg argues for the open communication, debate and dialogue common to traditional African culture. (39)

There is little doubt that South Africa's peaceful transition from apartheid into a non-racial democracy was secured, at least in part, by amazing communication tools and processes. From the Rustenburg Accord (Church leaders united for a new South Africa), to the Congress for the Democratisation of South Africa (Codesa), to the Truth and Reconciliation Commission (TRC), good communication was deployed, bringing real change and productivity to South Africa.

2. Team Man

The second team found in Genesis emerges as we read, "God created man in his own image, in the image of God He created him; male and female He created them" (Genesis 1:27; italics added). God gave the first Kingdom mandate, not to one individual, but to a couple, a family. Several team characteristics and reminders are evident in the Team Man.

Firstly, few relationships offer as clear an example of diversity as a husband and wife. The physical features alone warrant the description of opposites attracting. The differences continue into the sociological and psychological spheres. As noted by Daft, "Research has found that in general women tend to be more concerned with relationship building, inclusiveness, participation and caring." (40) No matter how the differences are categorised, they do exist and they are many.

Likewise, the role of diversity in team leadership cannot be overemphasised. As Paul said, "If the whole body were an eye, where would the hearing be? If the whole were hearing, where would the sense of smell be?" (I Corinthians 12:17). If everyone on the team is like everyone else, little productivity can occur. In *Teach your Team to Fish*, Laurie Beth Jones refers to homogenous groups as having "fewer arguments and worse answers". (41) Team productivity occurs within a unity of diversity, or, as van Rensburg notes, "The unity of humankind as well as its plurality and diversity are fundamental truths ... in the way we construct our social lives."

> **Diversity is not a goal, and it does not exist in a vacuum.**

Daft also notes that groups or teams with diversity tend to be more creative than homogenous groups. (42) The fact that God placed male and female together at the beginning of the creative mandate denotes the priority of diverse skills, gifts, perspectives and experiences. Nothing has changed since Jesus extended that mandate to disciple nations. The eclectic nature of his team, which included a tax collector, some fishermen, a physician and a former prosecutor, is noteworthy. The addition of women to his band of travellers was even more revealing, considering it was a male-dominated first-century culture.

Secondly, although diversity is critical to the team equation, it does not exist for its own sake. Diversity is not a goal, and it does not exist in a vacuum. Adam and Eve were created for the purpose of knowing God and filling the earth with productive change. Within a team context, diversity or differentiation has one primary objective, namely productivity. It finds purpose and meaning when it focuses on growth, or accomplishing a mission with others. Daft calls this the "paradox of diversity". (43) It is where apostolic leaders have to labour to unite others around a common purpose, while simultaneously honouring individual differences.

Few statements by the apostle Paul reflect the fruitfulness of this unique balance as, "From whom the whole body, being fitted and held together by what every joint supplies, according to the proper working of each individual part, causes the growth of the body" (Ephesians 4:16). One of the best contributions a leader can make within a team is to help others flourish, as well as find their fit. One of the key phrases adopted by our church leadership team in Johannesburg, South Africa over the years is, "We celebrate our diversity while embracing our unity." When diversity is embraced without unity towards a greater goal, teams fragment and lose their way.

Thirdly, Adam made a very revelatory statement concerning Eve. He said, "This is now bone of my bones" (Genesis 2:23). Put another way, "She may be different, but she came out of me." The fact that God formed Eve out of Adam highlights the necessity of self-awareness and personal mastery. Teams will be shaped by what is found in the character of a leader.

> **Teams will be shaped by what is found in the character of a leader.**

G. K. Chesterton was once invited to participate in an essay-writing contest. The title of the essay to be written was, "What is wrong with the world?" Chesterton's essay submission consisted of: "Dear Sirs, What is wrong with the world? I am. Yours Truly, G.K. Chesterton."

Ordering one's personal life is a non-negotiable criterion for apostolic team leadership. As Paul said, "I discipline my body and make it my slave, so that, after I have preached to others, I myself will not be disqualified" (I Corinthians (9:27). Van Rensburg calls self-awareness the foundation for personal mastery, while Daft refers to it as the "basis of all other competencies". (44)

Of course, self-awareness, which includes an awareness of our strengths and weaknesses, as well as the ability to recognise and understand our emotions and how they affect others, cannot happen in isolation. (45) Our experiences with God and with others not like us create the process of discovery and change.

Under the leadership of Ignatius Loyola, the intrepid Jesuits embraced self-awareness as one of the most critical skills for navigating changing and challenging environments. Author of Heroic Leadership and former Jesuit, Chris Lowney, noted that, prior to the Jesuits, most religious orders sought personal reflection and transformation within the safety of the cloister walls. Jesuit founder Loyola tore down the monastery walls and immersed the Jesuits in the maelstrom of daily life. (46) Their attention to self-awareness and personal development was a ubiquitous part of Jesuit accomplishments.

Daft calls this a high internal locus of control. (47) They believe that their attitudes, behaviour and actions are a greater determinant of what happens to them than any outside forces. Of course, the writer of Proverbs said it best, "Watch over your heart with all diligence, for from it flow the springs of life" (Proverbs 4:23). Fourthly, in Genesis 2:18, God said, "I will make him a helper suitable for him." Besides the emphasis on needing partners, the point about being suitable, or having an appropriate fit, should not be overlooked in any team environment.

> **Interestingly, his first step is not vision or strategy, but having the right people.**

In this context, the idea that people are the greatest resource in partnerships or teams needs a slight adjustment. In Good to Great, Jim Collins highlights the process of going from being a good company to a great company. Interestingly, his first step is not vision or strategy, but having the right people. He says the good-to-great leaders begin transformation by getting the right people on the bus and the wrong people off. (48) Not all leaders are suitable to the team, its mission or its relationships.

This is also reflected in the Biblical notion of grace-based leadership. As Paul said, "God has allotted to each a measure of faith," and "all the members do not have the same function" (Romans 12:3–4). He went on to write, "Since we have gifts that differ according to the grace given to us, each of us is to exercise them accordingly" (Romans 12:6). A position, title or job description will never do what only the grace given by God can do.

Of course, knowing who those right people are is no easy task. There are many factors that can influence fit within a team, such as individual personalities, cultural background and life experiences, but from our text in Genesis, suffice it to say that sharing core values and a common purpose, coupled with complementary skills, abilities and approaches, are trustworthy criteria for finding a suitable fit among team members.

3. Team God and Man

This third team is found in Genesis 3, where God comes to be with Adam and Eve in the Garden. The partnership between God and man is by far the most critical element within an apostolic leadership culture and any subsequent teams. In *Connecting,* a ground-breaking approach to psychotherapy, Dr Larry Crabb argues that self-awareness and self-discipline, although critical to personal development, have been overplayed by many Christians. He says knowing yourself and making good decisions must acquiesce to the nature of God in man. He writes, "The absolute centre of what He does to help us change is to reveal Himself to us, to give us a taste of what He's really like, and to pour his life into us." (49)

Following are a few more helpful insights that can assist team performance.
Firstly, the ability to see the good among the bad is critical in any relationship. If there is one thing that God adds to the relational equation, it is seeing bigger and better. Dr Crabb refers to "spiritual direction as recognising what God is up to in someone's life and joining the process". (50) Is it possible that this is one reason why Jesus could keep Judas on his leadership team, in spite of the fact that He knew that Judas was a thief, a liar and a betrayer?

When Jesus said that He only did what He saw the Father doing, it implies a capacity for seeing beyond someone's shortcomings. Paul pointed to this truth when he said, "Therefore from now on we recognise no one according to the flesh" (2 Corinthians 5:16). This statement was in the context that "the love of Christ controls us" (ibid. v. 14).

Paul's admonition to the Philippians, "whatever is true ... honourable ... right ... pure ... lovely ... of good repute ... if there is any excellence ... anything worthy of praise, dwell on these things" (Philippians 4:8) is made possible because of our partnership with God. He is the only one who can make "all things to work together for good" (Romans 8:28).

A consortium of universities did a comprehensive study for the purpose of discovering the secret to having a happy marriage. After all the research, only one common factor emerged. The husband viewed the wife in a more positive light than she saw herself, and vice versa. The term, positive allusions, was given to describe the attribute that these happy marriages possessed.

The idea of less becoming more always emerges.

Where the Pharisees only saw a despised chief tax gatherer, Zaccheus, Jesus saw "a son of Abraham" longing to break out of the materialistic box (Luke 19:1–11). Few leaders have demonstrated this quality as prolifically as former South African President, Nelson Mandela. Even though the Afrikaner people were his jailers, and the architects and operators of the apartheid system, Mandela had a special heart for the Afrikaner, according to G.J. Gerwel, Director General of the Office of the President during Mandela's Presidency. Gerwel said, "He (Mandela) genuinely believes that human beings are essentially good-doing beings." (51) That magnanimous perspective made him one of history's best reconcilers.

Secondly, the fact that God didn't start with a large multitude, but with just two individuals, underscores the significance of going small to go big. From "a cloud as small as a man's hand" (1 Kings 18:44) to the "five loaves and two fish" (Matthew 14:17), the idea of less becoming more always emerges. According to Jesus, what qualifies someone to be faithful with more comes through faithfulness in the little (Luke 16:10). Herein lays the quality known as focus.

Andy Stanley calls it "doing the few things well". (52) In the movie *The Patriot* Mel Gibson (the father) tells his young sons just before they ambush a group of British soldiers, "Aim small, miss small." The whole body is a big target, but to make it your aim is to potentially miss it completely. How many leaders and teams have missed the target, simply because it was too big? With so many opportunities and organisational tools handy, leaders and their teams must resist the temptation to want to do it all.

In *Simple Church*, Rainer and Geiger make a thought-provoking argument for simplicity. They advocate a four-element process that will de-clutter and invigorate the busy, but lifeless church. The last, but not least important element in their design process is "focus". (53) It is being able to say "no" to almost anything. They refer to it as the most difficult element to implement.

Although Rainer and Geiger have applied the principle of focus to building healthy churches, its application to any team is equally valid. Once we understand what we are called to do, with whom and how, everything else should be aligned with it. As a husband and a father, as a builder of a family, I eliminate anything from my life that would detract from the health and development of my family. The same should be true for a mission-directed team.

Thirdly, God asked a series of questions. Of course, it was for Adam and Eve's benefit, since He already knew the answers. The fact that God asked questions, rather than going straight to the problem or the solution is quite revealing. In *Leadership: A Communication Perspective*, Hackman and Johnson note that groups are more likely to make good decisions when the most influential members facilitate dialogue by asking questions. (54)

Asking powerful questions was a regular part of Jesus' teaching style and discipleship process. Albert Einstein once remarked, "If I had an hour to solve a problem and my life depended on the solution, I would spend the first 55 minutes determining the proper question to ask, for once I know the proper question, I could solve the problem in less than five minutes."

Much of our schooling focuses on the memorisation of answers, rather than the reasoning skills of enquiry.

According to Vogt, Brown and Isaacs, one of the primary hindrances to asking better questions, oddly enough, is the West's preoccupation with having the right answers. They state, "Western culture, and North American society in particular, focuses on having the right answers rather than discovering the right questions." (55) Much of our schooling focuses on the memorisation of answers, rather than the reasoning skills of enquiry. Vogt, Brown and Isaacs argue, "Questions open the door to dialogue and discovery. They are an invitation to creativity and breakthrough thinking. Questions can lead to movement and action on key issues; by generating creative insights, they can ignite change." (56)

Interestingly, in spite of Adam and Eve's enormous failure and its consequences, God's questions led to personal awareness and the initiation of creative change. In the midst of some painful realisations by Adam and Eve, God told the serpent, "I will put enmity ... between your seed and her seed; He shall bruise you on the head, and you shall bruise him on the heel" (Genesis 3:15). This highlights our first point about God revealing something good in any situation, and it reflects the innovative nature of partnering with God. An apostolic leadership culture is a place where positive change can be realised, no matter how adverse the conditions may be.

Conclusion

Patrick Lencioni calls real teamwork powerful and rare. Why rare? Possibly because, according to Katzenbach and Smith, every team is a group, but not every working group is a high-performance team. Katzenbach and Smith make their distinction around results. For them, the team is judged by joint outcomes, while those in working groups are judged more by individual performance.

> **A plurality of leaders functioning in a group is not necessarily the same as apostolic synergy towards the goal of bringing in the Kingdom.**

A plurality of leaders functioning in a group is not necessarily the same as apostolic synergy towards the goal of bringing in the Kingdom. Of course, Hackman and Johnson note that a leadership group does share the overall mission of the organisation and "measures its effectiveness by how well the organisation does". (57)

I agree with John Maxwell when he says, "Teams come in all shapes and sizes. If you are married, you and your spouse are a team. If you are employed by an organisation, you and your colleagues are a team. If you volunteer your time, you and your fellow workers are a team." (58) Regardless of the distinction, the point remains that team leadership is a combination of individual and group performance towards a shared purpose or goal.

In rebuilding Jerusalem, Nehemiah's team highlighted the contribution of diverse people, skills and gifts within the overall mission of transforming the city. Contained within this mission-directed team model were qualities critical to its success. It was a God-initiated work around the shared purpose of restoring Jerusalem. They depended upon a diversity of complementary skills, effective communication, clearly defined strategy, vulnerability-based trust and flexibility.

When developing an apostolic culture for effective transformation, team leadership should take its lead from principles and patterns revealed in Scripture. The Genesis model highlights the value and primary purpose of team leadership. It is a matter of fundamental design, where productivity through diversity, personal development, focus, fit and enquiry results from partnering with God.

In Chapter Five, we will look at how this Kingdom culture stimulates productive transformation through creativity and innovation within a global mind-set.

Discussion Questions

4.1 How would you describe an effective team?
4.2 What leadership teams are you currently part of, and what are some of the most effective aspects of these teams?
4.3 Identify some of the most essential principles of an effective team. Name examples from Scripture that reflect these truths.
4.4 Considering the vital qualities of a healthy team, what improvements need to be made in your current team/s?

CHAPTER FIVE

Global and Innovative

As discussed in Chapter One, gaining new territory is a ubiquitous feature among apostolic leaders and the Kingdom culture they develop. Of course, that new ground is comprised of both geographical expansion and social impact. It's the ability to bring the Kingdom of God into diverse environments and cultures.

One of the prevailing characteristics of an apostolic people is pioneering new territories for the purpose of transformation. In his book *Transformation* Ed Silvoso makes a distinction between discipling a nation and just ministering to people. (1)

For the early church, planting churches was a strategy, but reaching and impacting entire nations was the goal. The church at Antioch, the Apostle Paul's home base, was a fountainhead from where most of the expansion into the nations took place. Its culturally diverse and globally focused community became a launching pad into various nations. Paul's three missionary journeys were launched

> **For the early church, planting churches was a strategy, but reaching and impacting entire nations was the goal.**

from this city. Equally significant is the manner of that expansion. Engaging diverse cultures, environments and conditions required adjustments in how ministry was done and transformation achieved. Cannistraci notes how apostolic churches "develop and adapt to changing circumstances" without losing their essential nature and mission. (2)

101

Although the Kingdom message remained intact, i.e. proclaiming Christ and his reign in all spheres of life, the strategies and structures employed by Paul were adaptive and innovative. From Antioch to Macedonia, from Jerusalem to Athens, and then on to Rome, Paul demonstrated the Gospel's reach and relevance.

Interestingly, his home church in Antioch was the place where the disciples were first called "Christians". The word, disciple, is translated from the Greek word, mathetes, meaning learner. It was generally applied to anyone who followed a teacher, like the followers of John the Baptist or the Pharisees. The word Christian is derived from the Greek word, christianos, which comes from christos. The word, christos, or Christ, means anointed or anointed one.

Although the term, Christian, was first used as a form of ridicule, it implied something very new. A Christian was not just a follower of Jesus' teachings, but someone who was anointed as He was. Is it possible that this new way of classifying or identifying the followers of Christ contributed to Antioch's expansion and impact among the Gentiles? Wouldn't the identity of being anointed produce more change than just following the anointing?

> **A Christian was not just a follower of Jesus' teachings, but someone who was anointed as He was.**

The innovation of addressing the Greeks and not just the Jews, the rapid advance of the Gospel into Gentile cities, and the elimination of the legalism of the Judaizers were just a few of the significant contributions that Antioch's apostolic leaders and their Kingdom culture made to Christendom. Common to an apostolic leadership culture are global or multicultural competencies, as well as a steady supply of innovative strategies, structures and/or tools. This chapter examines the global/multicultural nature of apostolic leadership and the changes it brings. It also highlights qualities in African culture that are favourable towards that end.

From Paul to the Jesuits to the Reformation

The Apostle Paul, in his letter to the Romans, explained why he was delayed in visiting Rome:
And thus I aspired to preach the gospel, not where Christ was already named, so

that I would not build on another man's foundation; but as it is written, 'They who had no news of Him shall see, and they who have not heard shall understand.' For this reason I have often been prevented from coming to you. (Romans 15:20-22, italics added).

It may seem odd that the apostle to the Gentiles had yet to visit Rome, the capital of the Gentile world. However, the priority of going into unreached regions was a hallmark of Paul's apostleship. Paul's ability to reach and relate to people from different cultural spheres was notable. When he said, "I have become all things to all men, so that I may by all means save some" (1 Corinthians 9:22), he was emphasising his adaptive and innovative nature. He later told the Corinthians that, in order to seek "the profit of the many" (1 Corinthians 10:33), he must "please all men in all things".

> **Paul's approach was to customise (make to fit), not compromise.**

Paul's approach was to customise (make to fit), not compromise. The Greek word for please is aresko, which is derived from aro, meaning to fit, to adapt to. It's interesting to note that Paul referred to himself as a Pharisee, in order to gain support from the Pharisees during his defence before the Council in Jerusalem (Acts 23).

Paul's unique ability to adapt and innovate stood out at the Areopagus in Athens. Even though Paul's rhetoric was usually counterculture (language that "evokes the creation of a better society and a new future"), he started off with dominant culture rhetoric, i.e. he spoke in a culturally relevant manner to the Athenians. (3) He used their spiritual beliefs as an avenue towards salvation. It is highly unlikely that Paul would have made such a prolific impact if it hadn't been for this quality. Expanding the reach of the Kingdom into diverse geographical locations and social spheres is distinctly apostolic, and requires skills that make leaders relatable and relevant. In *Apostolic Strategies Affecting Nations*, Jonathan David underscored this unique apostolic quality when he wrote, "The apostolic ministry possesses a pioneering anointing; it is able to bulldoze into virgin territory and open up new frontiers." (4) Church history is replete with Christian leaders who have pushed the envelope both territorially and innovatively.

In the 16th century, the Jesuits demonstrated this remarkable ability. Ignatius Loyola didn't merely exhort his followers to be adaptable and creative; he tore down the monastery walls and thrust the Jesuits into the maelstrom of foreign cultures. (5) Unlike the Benedictines who valued stability, the Jesuits were committed to mobility and advancement. Their apostolic prowess was demonstrated by their capacity to innovate, remain flexible, adapt constantly, set ambitious goals, think globally, move quickly and take risks.

Lowney noted, "As confidants to European monarchs, China's Ming emperor, the Japanese shogun, and the Mughal emperor in India, the Jesuits boasted of a rolodex unmatched by that of any commercial, religious, or government entity." (6) Their pioneering abilities went far beyond launching communities of faith in unreached regions.

Accomplishments in languages, mathematics and the sciences were just a few of the Jesuits' many innovations. In just 10 years, they successfully launched 30 colleges and schools of higher learning around the world. Their dedication to higher education saw 700 secondary schools and colleges functioning by the late 18th century. (7)

Parallel to the apostolic exploits of the Jesuits was the transformational impact of the Protestant Reformation. Fuelled by the turbulence of three sitting Popes, a provocative Augustine monk named Martin Luther, and the restoration of the priesthood of the believer, the Protestant Reformation launched a new season of apostolic ministry. (8) The changes and

It moved the Church from ritual and formula to faith and relationships.

innovations, which eventually became known as Protestant practices, affected everything from music and worship service times to the very structure of the sanctuary. It moved the Church from ritual and formula to faith and relationships.

The Reformation led away from a rigid Episcopalian model of governance and added more pastoral and Presbyterian processes. It challenged the medieval feudal system, and led to democratic and representative thought. Like the "New Apostolic Reformation" of the 1990s, the Protestant Reformation nailed its colours to the mast of "sola scriptura, scriptura sola". Coupled with the priesthood of every believer, Scripture only liberated masses of Christians from restrictive religious hierarchies.

Personal responsibility and empowerment marked this epic period. Modern science as a discipline is a fruit of this apostolic season. As Francis Bacon, the father of the scientific method, once put it: "There are two books laid before us to study; to prevent us falling into error; first, the volume of the Scriptures which reveal the will of God; then the volume of his creation, which express his power." (9) As we fast-forward hundreds of years, we find apostolic ministry unchanged from its original mandate, and unrelenting in fostering territorial growth and transformational change.

P.W. Wagner notes how most denominations are heritage-focused, whereas apostolic ministries are future-focused (10). Denominational leaders tend to favour the past and maintenance, whereas apostles lead towards the future by implementing changes in how and where ministry is done.

Wagner calls the resurgence of the apostolic in the 1990s the "most radical change in the way of doing church since the Protestant Reformation." (11) It encompasses changes in names, authority structures, leadership training, ministry focuses, worship styles, prayer forms, financing and outreach. Wagner views this apostolic season as "changing the shape of protestant Christianity around the world." (12)

Wagner views this apostolic season as 'changing the shape of protestant Christianity around the world'.

The current growth of churches in Africa, Asia and Latin America is considered by some experts to be a missiological phenomenon. (13) This new apostolic surge has found favourable conditions around the globe; few more favourable than the multicultural qualities found in Africa/South Africa.

Global Competencies and Africa

In spite of its chequered leadership track record, Africa has no shortage of apostolic leaders who stand out as models of cross-cultural competence and innovative change. From the adventures of the intrepid David Livingstone in southern and central Africa to the courageous exploits of Roland and Heidi Baker in Mozambique, a demonstration of cross-cultural leadership abounds in Africa.

105

For Dr Livingstone, it meant, "The end of the geographical feat is only the beginning of the missionary enterprise" (14) and for Roland and Heidi Baker it means serving "the very poor: the destitute, the lost, the broken, and the forgotten." (15)

From Albert Schweitzer's work at Lamberene in Equatorial Africa to Mahatma Gandhi's formative years in South Africa, we see a model of leadership character and competence emerging that successfully traverses cultural and national boundaries. From South Africa's Nelson Mandela to Ghana's Kofi Annan, we find a portrait of leadership that's formed in African culture and fashioned for global achievement.

Africa is no stranger to leaders who have transcended cultural boundaries and changed nations. Gandhi once said, "I was born in India but I was made in South Africa." (16) He credits the lion's share of his leadership development and the subsequent success of the Satyagraha method (devotion to the truth), which contributed significantly to India's liberation from colonial rule, to his years of experience in South Africa's early civil rights movement.

On arriving in South Africa, he called himself a "dull boy who couldn't put two sentences together". Yet, when he left the country, he was an inspiring leader — fearless, selfless and with a vision that changed the socio-political landscape of India. The challenges of South Africa's multicultural context had a transformational impact on Gandhi. He learnt bridge-building in the trenches of African culture.

He learnt bridge-building in the trenches of African culture.

The African environment, with its diverse cultures, peoples and experiences, provides multiple opportunities for contributing to the development of global and transformational competencies, such as self-awareness through experience and diversity. Equally noteworthy is that Africa as a continent reflects a solidarity that is capable of partnering across multiple national boundaries. That solidarity emanates from both its cultural peculiarities and its shared histories.

As a continent, does Africa have its own culture? Are there patterns of thought and behaviour that are uniquely African; and can they become an advantage in developing global leaders who foster effective and sustainable transformation?

In *The Spirit of African Leadership*, Professor Lovemore Mbigi noted that, in spite of the domination of colonial powers during the first half of the 20th century, African culture remains a centrifugal force. Although every African country has its own unique culture, as does their many unique ethnic groups, there are commonalities among them that are distinctly African. It is that commonality that apostolic leaders and their teams must understand, engage and leverage.

Mbigi echoed the significance of this point when he said, "The ultimate task of leadership in African organisations and communities is to develop intelligent cultural strategies rooted in African cultural belief systems and thought, so as to ensure sustainable development and transformation." (17) Professor B.J. van der Walt, author of *When African and Western Cultures Meet*, describes culture as an "integrated system of ideas, feelings

> **Africans have a thing called Ubuntu; it's the essence of being human, it is part of the gift that Africa is going to give to the world.**

and values and their associated patterns of behaviour and products shared by a group of people". (18) There are many social categories that reflect the unique ideas, feelings and values of African culture. Among them is the African philosophy of community or Ubuntu.

In African philosophy, the starting point is social relations. In his book *The Right to Hope: Global Problems, Global Vision* Archbishop Desmond Tutu put it best when he said, "Africans have a thing called Ubuntu; it's the essence of being human, it is part of the gift that Africa is going to give to the world." (19)

For an African, the individual is first and foremost a member of a community. Van Rensburg noted that an African will view himself as bound by a mutual obligation to consider others and the common good. (20) This African cultural peculiarity may be understood from a Xhosa proverb, "umuntu ngumuntu ngabantu", which translated, means, "a person is a person through persons". The Zulu derivative, Ubuntu, or simply, "I am because we are" places the identity, value and contribution of the individual squarely within the interests of the community. They are seen as inseparable.

Black, Morrison and Gregersen, in their work *Global Explorers* underscored the need for global leaders to connect emotionally with people within a broader community. (21) They said, "Because globalisation is built on the principle of integration, a leader who connects with people is particularly valuable." (22)

Quite frankly, when Connie and I first began working in southern Africa, it was our ability to connect with almost anyone that made the difference between success and failure. Prior to our move to South Africa, the only mission experience we had outside the United States, was to Jamaica. The greatest asset we possessed, besides a word from God and the Holy Spirit, was our ability to relate to a great diversity of people. Connie and I had Ubuntu, even before we knew what it was. It is precisely through this African practice of Ubuntu that integration can be leveraged for building global partnerships in Africa and abroad. Kofi Annan's tenure as the seventh Secretary-General of the United Nations was noted for bringing the United Nations "closer to the people". His Nobel Peace Prize reflected a global capacity for promoting justice and peace. In his final speech as Secretary-General, he called for all countries to return to multilateral foreign policies, and to follow the credo, "The responsibility of the great states is to serve and not dominate the peoples of the world." (23)

> **For Mandela, to spew vengeance on one segment of society was to spew vengeance upon all.**

Annan promoted this Ubuntu ethic when he said, "In an age where community involvement and partnerships with civil society are increasingly being recognised as indispensable, there is clearly a growing potential for co-operative development and renewal worldwide." Ubuntu provided the basis for Nelson Mandela's rejection of retribution against the perpetrators of apartheid crimes, and paved the way for South Africa's subsequent recovery.

Archbishop Desmond Tutu explained the reason when he said, "The humanity of the perpetrator of apartheid atrocities was caught up and bound up in that of his victim whether he liked it or not." (24) In other words, what was done to some was done to all. For Mandela, to spew vengeance on one segment of society was to spew vengeance upon all. His deep commitment to the brotherhood of all men modelled the way for old enemies to "beat their swords into ploughshares". (25)

What global leadership competencies have emerged from this Ubuntu ethic and how do they influence transformation?

McCall and Hollenbeck noted that the crossing of cultural lines will assault the identity of an individual; this is where basic assumptions about our lives are realised and questioned. (26) This is where transformation can take place of who we are and how we see ourselves and others.

Robert Greenleaf notes that awareness is not a giver of solace; it is just the opposite (27). It is a disturber and an awakener. For example, in the parable of the Good Samaritan, the Samaritan was disturbed by the dreadful condition of another human being. He was awakened to what was similar and different between himself and the injured man. It provoked new things, both for himself and the other man. This is the principle and power of identification, where we see and understand ourselves in relation to another human being. It is a psychological orientation of self towards another, leading to strong emotional attachment and change.

While identity is who we actually are, our distinguishing character and personality, identification is the capacity to see ourselves in who someone else is. It enables us to recognise what is similar and different, resulting in strong emotional association and corresponding action.

> **While identity is who we actually are, our distinguishing character and personality, identification is the capacity to see ourselves in who someone else is.**

Unlike the Levite and priest, the Samaritan got close enough to see beyond the culturally imposed boundary of "Jews have no dealings with Samaritans". Hall, Zhu and Yan propose identity and adaptability as meta-competencies or underlying abilities needed for learning from experience. They say, "We know that these deep changes in personal identity occur as a result of being confronted with a higher level of complexity in the environment ... i.e., the ability to see the situation through another person's eyes is a quality of a more evolved identity." (28)

The Samaritan demonstrated this quality by doing for the injured man what he would need and expect for himself. He was having an Ubuntu moment; his state was directly connected to the condition of the other man. Ubuntu inspires us to expose ourselves to others; to encounter the difference of their humanness, so as to inform and enrich our own. (29)

As John Maxwell described it, "Instead of putting others in their place put yourself in their place." The accolade of Good Samaritan denotes a transformational moment. McCall and Hollenbeck said, "At some point a fundamental transformation takes place ... a transformation that can be described as the acquisition of a global mind-set." (30) According to B.J. van der Walt, the individual who has Ubuntu is always open and available to others. It's about understanding oneself more fully by understanding others. (31)

Expanding on Descartes' proposition of, "I think, therefore I am," Ubuntu emphasises self through community by proposing, "I am because I belong." Ubuntu places this kind of self-awareness squarely in the context of experience and diversity.

> **John Maxwell described it, "Instead of putting others in their place put yourself in their place."**

Mobley and McCall pose an important question: "If a global mind-set is a combination of competencies that enable one to work across cultural boundaries, how does the mind-set develop?" (32) According to their research, experience is the primary vehicle for developing global leadership skills. They note that cross-cultural experiences are well known for developing cultural awareness. (33)

It didn't take Jesus much time before He was sending his disciples off to other cities and regions in Israel (Luke 10:1). He was keenly aware of the impact their travels and encounters would have on their own lives. After their return, Jesus told them that they had seen and heard things that prophets and kings long to see and hear (Luke 10:24).

Was it simply going out into unfamiliar territory that brought the change? This begs the question, "Are all cross-cultural experiences the same?" Would touring the castles of historical Europe have the same transformational impact as doing a year of service in an African hospice or a Kenyan orphanage? Would daily rides on the tube in London, over a two-week holiday, provide the same learning opportunities as two months along the Zambezi River with only Zimbabweans for company?

Certainly, Peter had experiences with Roman soldiers prior to his transformational encounter at Cornelius's household (Acts 10). Morgan McCall says, "Though most people emerge from the vast majority of their experiences unchanged in any significant way, some experiences do have a significant impact on one's understanding of oneself, one's view of the world, one's sense of right and wrong, and one's subsequent behaviour." (34) This suggests, "All experiences are not equal."

In 500 BC, Heraclitus, in his quest to understand the ways of nature, concluded that all learning comes through strife. In other words, challenging experiences produce new learning opportunities. Few experiences are more challenging than engaging another culture for the first time. The term, culture shock, was first coined in 1960 by anthropologist Kalvero Oberg to represent the amount of anxiety experienced by the loss of one's identity in the face of new cultural shifts. Since that time, it has been extensively studied, and is now used to identify the developmental experiences in another culture.

Living the Ubuntu ethic creates an attitude and an environment of co-operation where these developmental experiences can abound. It prevents an isolationist attitude and makes the interaction between diverse cultures second nature. The growing number of agreements between African states and global powers reflects this point. Beyond the geo-political complexities, the capacity of African leaders to engage simultaneously with Western and Eastern nations, in spite of those countries having conflicting ideological positions, is indicative of the cross-cultural reach of Ubuntu.

> **In other words, challenging experiences produce new learning opportunities.**

As Kenneth Kaunda, former president of Zambia said, "Our people enjoy other people for their own sakes; they are patient, forgiving, accepting and inclusive." (35) There is a significant degree of uncertainty and anxiety that coalesces within the Ubuntu environment. Its very nature engages the pressures of diversity; and as Joseph Campbell notes, "The essence of development is that diversity and adversity beat out repetition every time." (36) Real change or innovation happens when the pressures of diversity are met head-on. Few apostolic leaders have reflected this point as profoundly as the indomitable Apostle Paul.

A Pauline Model for Global Competence

Paul's rhetoric to the believers in Rome demonstrates his level of self-awareness, in relationship to the socio-cultural realities of Rome. His letter to the church in Rome is his longest, and considered to be among the last to be written. Unlike Paul's letters to the Galatians or the Corinthians, his letter to the Roman Christians was in preparation for his very first visit. In Paul's Letter to the Romans, Ben Witherington notes, "Paul must pick and choose his words carefully ... knowing that first impressions are important." (37) Paul was building relational foundations and a social network, in preparation for both his message and his visit.

He began the letter with his own story, i.e. "Paul, a bond-servant of Christ Jesus, called as an apostle, set apart for the gospel of God ..." (Romans 1:1). Paul had little to no relational history with the church in Rome. Notably, his first challenge was to establish his credentials with those who were not his converts. Although Paul had significant credentials as a Roman citizen and a former Pharisee with a Greek education, he was reluctant to use this as clout when first entering a new situation. He did not appeal to his own illustrious past as a Jew as he'd done elsewhere.

He first introduced himself as a slave of Jesus Christ. Paul's emphasis on being a slave of Christ challenged Roman Imperialism, which in Mediterranean society was the known world order. Noteworthy is the fact that there were more slaves in Rome than freemen. It is likely that the majority of Roman Christians were either slaves or former slaves. It is unlikely that Paul's largely Gentile audience would have been familiar with the Old Testament concept of the prophets of God being servants. Paul's understanding and reference to his role as a servant, reflects awareness of both the heart of cross-cultural leadership and the unique context of the Roman believers. Dictators didn't build Rome, servants did.

Dictators didn't build Rome, servants did.

According to Robert Greenleaf, servant leadership is the more able and less able serving of each other, and becomes the rock on which a good society is built. He says, "It helps others to a larger and nobler vision and purpose." (38) Herein lies the key to breaching barriers in sub-Saharan Africa — servant leadership. Although traditional African leadership centres on the concept of kingship, this is not the autocratic dictatorship experienced during colonial and post-colonial times. Rather, the king was a servant to the clan, tribe and community.

Commenting on African traditions in leadership, Gerhard van Rensburg notes, "Leadership is built from the foundation of service to the community to the level where the chief is custodian of the community." (39) Early African societies were more participatory and democratic. According to Mulemfo, leaders were considered facilitators, as well as servants within the community. (40) They worked with the whole community when making traditional law.

It is interesting to note that, according to the GLOBE study (Global Leadership and Organisational Behaviour Effectiveness Research Programme), sub-Saharan Africa ranked among the highest for humane-orientated leadership (the well-being of followers being the focus), which, according to Winston and Ryan, is the leadership archetype most favourable for servant leadership. (41)

Although the incidence of humane-oriented practices is very low in places like Nigeria, in West Africa, the fact that sub-Saharan Africa had the highest humane-orientation value score helps to explain why it is more conducive to servant leadership. (42) After more than 25 years of living and labouring in sub-Saharan Africa, I can honestly say, without hesitation, that those who have served the best have accomplished the most. Jesus knew what He was saying when He declared, "Whoever wishes to become great among you shall be your servant" (Matthew 20:26).

Jesus, who was without question the quintessential global leader, said, "The Son of Man did not come to be served, but to serve, and to give his life a ransom for many" (Matthew 20:28). From the global exploits of the Apostle Paul and the early church to apostolic leaders in the 21st century, adapting and innovating for continued development and progress are familiar features. New and improved strategies and structures have emerged from within this apostolic climate and culture.

The Apostle Paul's receiving a vision to go to Macedonia (Europe) had ground-breaking impact. Taking the Gospel to the Gentiles was a new strategy, while launching the Church in the household of a businesswoman named Lydia was a significant first. Paul, who was strategic in choosing his bases of operation, selected the home of a respected woman. It should be noted that Macedonia was more advanced than most areas in the ancient world regarding the respect given to women.

According to Cannistraci, this first house church was established by a group of praying women at Philippi; hardly a model of either Jerusalem or Antioch. (43) Also, the church in Rome was very different from that of Jerusalem, Antioch or Ephesus. There were no central organisational structures. Witherington notes that there were various house churches with no centralised leadership structure. (44)

In spite of his leadership roles in Antioch and Ephesus, there is no evidence that Paul attempted to restructure the church in Rome according to those models, albeit he did use strong rhetoric designed to unite Jewish and Gentile Christians. (45) The fact that God gave no structural blueprint for what a local church should look like, helps apostolic leaders avoid the temptations of organisational cloning. Organisational structure must be shaped by the function of Kingdom life and purpose relative to different environments.

> **I can honestly say, without hesitation, that those who have served the best have accomplished the most.**

Dee Hock, founder of VISA, and author of *The Birth of the Chaordic Age*, poignantly stated, "Purpose and principle, clearly understood and articulated, and commonly shared, are the genetic code of any healthy organisation. To the degree that you hold purpose and principles in common among you, you can dispense with command and control. People will know how to behave in accordance with them, and they will do it thousands of unimaginable, creative ways. The organisation will become a vital, living set of beliefs." (46)

Since the beginning of his earthly ministry until now, Jesus and his apostolic leaders have used relevant strategies and flexible structures suitable for bringing the Kingdom of God into diverse social environments. For over 2 000 years, Jesus has been building his Church. Century after century, the Church has grown in a variety of ways. It grew one way in New Testament times, and another way in the Roman Empire before Constantine. It

> **Flexibility and innovation are essential apostolic qualities.**

grew one way during the Protestant Reformation, and another way in the Chinese underground. It's growing one way among African independent churches and another way in Latin American "grassroots churches". (47)

The strategies and structures of apostolic ministry have adjusted to changing conditions like a new wineskin adapts to the expansion of new wine. In *Organic Church: Growing Faith Where Life Happens*, Neil Cole argues for Kingdom expansion based on sowing seed everywhere: in coffeehouses, campuses, businesses, homes, bars, clubs and hospitals. He says, "Why start coffeehouses to attract lost people? Why not just go to the coffeehouse where they already are?" (48) Flexibility and innovation are essential apostolic qualities.

From new modes of governing, which vested greater authority in apostolic leaders, as well as empowered congregants, to decentralised church structures, where the benchmark of Christian community moved from Sunday attendance to small groups, the way of doing ministry broke traditional ranks. The Church is far more than just an organisation. It is an organism; living, changing and growing. Rather than being frozen in time, it develops and adapts to changing circumstances, while retaining its essential nature and mission.

The ability to customise, but not compromise, is uniquely apostolic, and new strategies and structures are not for their own sake, but for the purpose of advancing the Kingdom. This pattern is playing out through multiple strategies and structures such as house churches, cell churches, seeker-friendly churches, simple churches, online Christian communities, multi-site churches, the emergent church movement, cross-sector collaboration, networks and alliances.

> **Within an apostolic leadership culture, strategies and structures adapt to fit the scope of the Kingdom mission, as well as changing environmental factors.**

Rather than simply following traditional models and systems to maintain organisational stability, apostles and apostolic teams look for the most effective ways to lead change and bring transformation. Within an apostolic leadership culture, strategies and structures adapt to fit the scope of the Kingdom mission, as well as changing environmental factors. A design model conducive to producing apostolic strategy and structure is found in Robert Keidel's "Triadic Framework." It reflects a more robust or full-bodied perspective towards change; one that suits an apostle's approach to growth. (49)

In *Seeing Organizational Patterns*, Keidel argues that "there are only three ways in which people can relate." (50) Human relationships, as well as human organisations, are characterised by autonomy, control and co-operation. (51) This is where the capacities and competences of individuals coalesce and organise for productive purposes. Keidel purports that the blending of individuality, community and continuity explains a large portion of organisational design issues. (52)

The Apostle Paul captured this point metaphorically when he wrote, "The whole body, being fitted and held together by what every joint supplies, according to the proper working of each individual part" (Ephesians 4:16). In other words, Paul was basing the growth of the Church on this triadic model, where unique and diverse individuals fit into strategic partnerships and then organise towards sustainable growth.

On the subject of South Africa's transformational ventures, Nelson Mandela echoed that same sentiment when he said, "Each and every South African needs to show a determination to work together and make our country a winning nation." (53) Effective three-variable thinking prioritises autonomy, co-operation and control, so that appropriate integration and trade-offs can be made. (54)

> **The addition of flexible autonomy, which was a novel approach in the first-century Mediterranean world, became a hallmark of the early church.**

The focus will depend on whichever variable(s) require attention at any given time. (55) For example, when Connie and I first launched out in South Africa, exercising our autonomy (individual gifts, decisions and effort) was vital for discovering new opportunities and relationships. As we began to develop community, more attention was given to suitable processes and structures.

The addition of flexible autonomy, which was a novel approach in the first-century Mediterranean world, became a hallmark of the early church and a key advantage in its expansion throughout the Roman Empire. Although many early Christian gatherings began in the synagogues, houses became the primary unit of the Christian church (Acts 13, 14, 17, 18, 19).

In Romans 16, Paul's greetings and acclamation of many leaders, their house churches and labours illustrate this point. In like manner, an apostolic leadership culture generates a co-operation-based design, blending diverse leaders, multifunctional autonomous teams and horizontal decision-making. (56) South Africa's unique blend of African communalism and Western entrepreneurialism is more than suitable for effecting new co-operation-based strategies and structures. In *Ubuntu: An Ethic for a New South Africa*, Augustine Shutte contends that the blend of integration and differentiation found in the South African Ubuntu cultural ethic can make synthesis and change more prodigious and effective.(57) According to Gerhard van Rensburg, it builds an "environment of trust", where open communication, quality debate and consensus-building generate better decision-making and results. (58) It's where creative thinking is best stimulated and status quo practices are best challenged. Although not a new concept, among the most valuable strategies for developing an apostolic leadership culture and stewarding sustainable transformation are apostolic alliances and/or networks.

The Apostolic: New Alliances and Networks

Arguing for the connectivity of all things, and its impact on business, science and everyday life, Barabasi, in Linked, laments the dearth of understanding about life, as a whole. He says, "After spending trillions of research dollars to disassemble nature in the last century, we are just now acknowledging that we have no clue how to continue; except to take it apart further." (59)

He continues, "Most events and phenomena are connected, caused by, and interacting with a huge number of other pieces of a complex universal puzzle. We have come to see that we live in a small world, where everything is linked to everything else ...We have come to grasp the importance of networks." (60)

> **We have come to see that we live in a small world, where everything is linked to everything else.**

Commenting on the growth and impact of networks, Cannistraci notes, "Explosive advances are being made because people are connecting to increase the benefits for everyone. The trend is called networking and many agree that it is the wave of the future because it is so effective." (61) Networking is a natural by-product of an apostolic heart. Rather than acquiescing to denominational boundaries, true apostolic ministry has a vision for the entire Body of Christ, and relates to the Church as a broader community in a city. Developing an apostolic culture creates resistance against parochial tendencies found in much of Christendom today.

The isolating and polarising habits of fallen man were confronted by Paul when he wrote, "For when one says, 'I am of Paul,' and another, 'I am of Apollos,' are you not mere men?" (1 Corinthians 3:4) Paul equated that mind-set with being carnal or fleshly. The Greek words used for "flesh" are sarkino and sarx. They denote a material or one-dimensional approach to reality; a very limited and deficient perspective.

When the disciples told of their attempt to prevent someone from casting out a demon, simply because he was not part of their group, Jesus said, "Do not hinder him; for he who is not against you is for you" (Luke 9:50). Jesus was actually saying, "What we are doing is not restricted to our personal airspace." Jesus said that the Kingdom of Heaven is like a dragnet. The symbol of a net is enormously successful because of its thousands of connecting knots. It can cover a large area and pull in mass quantities of fish because of the strength of these knots. The knots represent strong partnerships capable of covering large areas.

> **This is where the Body of Christ moves from the emergence of apostles to the convergence of apostolic ministries.**

Today, the Kingdom net is expanding at an unprecedented rate. "Some researchers estimate that two to three new networks are being formed in Africa alone every day." (62) The magnitude of this apostolic season has reached a crescendo in the networking of networks. This is where the Body of Christ moves from the emergence of apostles to the convergence of apostolic ministries.

From the Network of Christian Ministries of the 1980s to the Revival Alliance of today, apostolic leaders have been forging broad-based Kingdom partnerships. From the International Federation of Christian Churches (IFCC) in South Africa to Global Legacy in the United States, churches and related ministries are carving out new alliances from the "compatibility of values, mission and doctrine". (63)

118

The cross-pollination of diverse apostolic movements can make the discipling of nations a greater likelihood in our generation. "Once Kingdom networks begin to network, the possible advantages for the Church become enormous. When the Body of Christ reaches this level, entire nations can be taken, as they were in the early decades of the Church." (64) This apostolic ability to gather and unite is not just ministerial fellowship. Its purpose is to bring the Kingdom through strategically aligned relationships and Spirit-empowered believers.

For over 25 years, Connie and I have experienced first-hand the power of this apostolic quality. Our arrival and ministry in South Africa could not have happened without the support of unrelated ministries and churches already functioning here. If Ray McCauley, founder and Senior Pastor of the Rhema Church in Johannesburg, had not offered his ministry as a doorway into the nation, we may never have come.

Our current Africa-wide ministry began with networking. From inception to maturity, the road was paved with timely alliances. Early on in our African journey, we partnered with other apostolic leaders and their movements, such as Costa Mitchell of the Vineyard churches, and Tony Fitzgerald of Church of the Nations. Apostolic leaders like Tom Deuschle from Zimbabwe became key contributors to our development and growth.

In 1992, it was our alliance with Pastor Paul Daniel and His People Church in Cape Town that was instrumental in us creating the new nation-building tool, known as SYMSA (Symposium for the Biblical Reformation of South Africa). This fuelled a nationwide movement towards

> **From inception to maturity, the road was paved with timely alliances.**

Biblically based transformation, and led to a brand-new wineskin (organisational structure), called His People Christian Churches.

From strategic alliances with organisations such as Every Nation Churches, and Regent University in Virginia Beach, Virginia, to more apostolic partners like Joe Martin from Dallas, Texas and Bill Johnson from Redding, California, the scale and scope of bringing the Kingdom to African soil has expanded exponentially.

Conclusion

One of the conspicuous characteristics of the early church was its speed in breaking away from the religious conventions of the day. They quickly moved from being temple or synagogue-centred, to being centred in houses and the marketplace.

Cannistraci notes how freedom from prevailing religious methods enabled creative thinking to "guide their activity", resulting in astonishing growth and expansion. (65) The Kingdom's geographically expansive and innovatively expressed nature has continued unabated for over 2 000 years, and the role of the apostolic has led the way.

From within an apostolic culture, cross-cultural competencies and ground-breaking capacities emerge. Among these competencies are self-awareness, identification and servant leadership, as developed and expressed within diverse environments and experiences. Within the tensions and uncertainties of new cultural experiences, a transformation takes place that is both personal and social. According to Robbins, the transformational nature of redemption emerges as believers adopt new attitudes, ideas, behaviour and practices. (66) For example, "Consider it all joy ... when you encounter various trials" (James 1:2) and "The brother of humble circumstances is to glory in his high position" (James 1:9) imply approaching difficulties with new attitudes and behaviour. Put another way, the trial is actually an ally ushering in new possibilities.

In his book *Positive Turbulence* Stanley Gryskiewics echoed this sentiment when he wrote, "That chaotic, swirling frenetic environment that threatens to drown us all is also where new trends are incubated." (67) The African environment, with its many cultural peculiarities, e.g. Ubuntu, opportunities and crises is an incubator for developing global competence.

As apostles and apostolic leaders continue their movement into new regions and cultures, the emerging Kingdom culture will engender creativity and innovation, leading to effective and sustainable transformation.

In the next chapter, we will examine another hallmark of an apostolic leadership culture. Spirit-filled enablement and renewal, and the presence of signs, wonders and miracles through Spirit-empowered believers are an indispensable part of bringing the Kingdom and generating sustainable transformation.

Discussion Questions

5.1 Give several benefits of being connected beyond a single geographical location or culture.

5.2 Why is it important to have relationships and labour outside one's local church or community?

5.3 What are some direct benefits that you have experienced in multicultural relationships?

5.4 Describe several new things you have implemented through your leadership over the past few years.

5.5 Describe the networks or alliances, if any, in which you are involved. Please highlight their direct and indirect advantages.

CHAPTER SIX

Spirit-filled Enablement and the Long Haul

From the early days of doing ministry on college campuses in the United States to our many leadership adventures in Africa, the presence of divine power and Spirit-filled enablement has been a constant companion. From the amazing healing of a partially crippled man at the University of Tennessee to countless salvations, deliverances, healings and miracles throughout South Africa, we have experienced firsthand what it means to bring a message that is not in persuasive words of human wisdom, "but in demonstration of the Spirit and of power" (1 Corinthians 2:4).

Equally significant is how much fresh faith and passion Connie and I still have after 30 years of intensive full-time Christian ministry. Considering the number of casualties among those in full-time Christian service, this is no small testimony. According to recent studies, thousands of pastors and other church leaders leave the ministry and their local churches every year. Dr Richard J. Krejcir calls the job of Christian ministry a "dangerous occupation". (1) An extensive study at the Francis A. Schaeffer Institute of Church Leadership Development found that 70 percent of pastors are so "stressed out and burned out that they regularly consider leaving the ministry". (2)

> **Dr. Richard J. Krejcir calls the job of Christian ministry a 'dangerous occupation'.**

Between 35 and 40 percent actually leave their churches within the first five years. The reasons and causes for leadership turnover in Christian organisations are many; some as innocuous as simple migration from one geographical location to another, and others as insidious as moral failure, bitter conflicts and abusive relationships.

Among the many reasons for leader turnover in Christian organisations is the issue of "burnout". Research distilled from Barna, Focus on the Family and Fuller Seminary revealed that about one in 500 pastors leave full-time ministry every month because of "moral failure, spiritual burnout and contention in their churches". (See full article in Addendum A, Burnout and Renewal in Christian Organisations.)

Although we have experienced the enormous pressures that accompany church planting, pastoring on challenging mission fields and navigating countless human tragedies, the Holy Spirit has been the "fourth" man in our fiery furnaces (Daniel 3:25). As Paul said, "... that He would grant you, according to the riches of His glory, to be strengthened with power through his Spirit in the inner man" (Ephesians 3:16).

Pastor Bill Johnson from the Bethel Church in Redding, California, calls the Holy Spirit the greatest gift ever received. He says the Holy Spirit is the agent of heaven that makes the incomprehensible possible because He is with us. (3) Is it any wonder that Jesus said that speaking "against the Son of Man" was forgivable, while speaking "against the Holy Spirit" was unforgivable? (Matthew 12:32). This statement followed the incident where the Pharisees ascribed the deliverance of a demon-possessed man to the work of the demonic.

Whether from ignorance, deception or hardness of heart, resisting the Person and work of the Holy Spirit is considered by Jesus to be the most egregious error.

Whether from ignorance, deception or hardness of heart, resisting the Person and work of the Holy Spirit is considered by Jesus to be the most egregious error. Since Jesus Himself is at the right hand of the Father, it is the Holy Spirit alone who brings and releases who Jesus is to his people.

Jesus told the disciples that it was to their "advantage" (John 16:7) that He was going away. In other words, the Holy Spirit would be their advantage in everything. Whether someone is an apostle or an astronaut, an evangelist or an engineer, the Holy Spirit is their greatest asset. R.A. Torrey, in *The Person and Work of the Holy Spirit*, argued that both spiritual life and "material being" are maintained and developed by the Holy Spirit. He said, "The development of the material universe into higher states of order is attributed to the agency of the Holy Spirit." (4)

Rather than being relegated to the sole function of spiritual mentor, the Holy Spirit is God's presence everywhere; revealing, releasing and demonstrating the Kingdom of God on earth as it is in heaven. From the prominence of the Holy Spirit in the lives and ministries of the early disciples to his work and impact in the Body of Christ today, it is evident that Spirit-filled power and enablement has been, and is, a non-negotiable quality for developing an apostolic leadership culture.

In *Whatever Happened to the Power of Go?*, Dr. Michael Brown posed some sobering questions. He asked, "Why do so many believers hear so many sermons, listen to so many teaching tapes, read so many faith-building books, follow so many formulas, make so many efforts to grow and never seem to change?" (5) Is this what life in the Spirit is all about?

A truly Spirit-filled community and culture is marked by amazing change and growth.

The answer is an unequivocal "no"! A truly Spirit-filled community and culture is marked by amazing change and growth.

What does the role and ministry of the Holy Spirit look like in an apostolic culture, and how does his ministry help leaders build for the long haul? What evidence is there of the Holy Spirit's work in the Church, and what can be done to burnout-proof leaders who labour to bring the Kingdom?

The Apostolic and the Holy Spirit

A simple perusal of the Book of Acts reveals a deeply personal relationship between the Holy Spirit and the Church. From Jesus' last message to his apostles, "You will receive power when the Holy Spirit has come upon you" (Acts 1:8), to Peter's first message promising the Holy Spirit to "all who are far off" (Acts 2:39), the essential nature of a relationship with the Holy Spirit is quite apparent.

In fact, the most life-changing feature throughout the Book of Acts is how the apostles and other leaders yielded to the presence, direction and action of the

Holy Spirit. For example, Peter's acceptance of Gentile conversion only occurred once he'd witnessed the outpouring of the Holy Spirit on Cornelius's family (Acts 10:44-47); and it was the Holy Spirit who prompted leaders in Antioch to send Barnabas and Paul to other nations (Acts 13:2).

Interestingly, Philip, who began as a server of food to widows, was led by the Holy Spirit to reach the first convert from Africa, the Ethiopian eunuch (Acts 8:26—27). In describing the partnership between Philip and the Holy Spirit, Luke wrote, "The Spirit of the Lord snatched Philip away" (Acts 8:39, Italics added). The Greek word for "snatch" is harpazo, meaning to seize. It is a derivative of aihreomai, meaning to take for oneself.

> **The most life-changing feature throughout the Book of Acts is how the apostles and other leaders yielded to the presence, direction and action of the Holy Spirit.**

This language denotes the apostolic nature of our relationship with the Holy Spirit. It signifies being called to Him, which becomes a catalyst for working with Him. Being and doing are mutually inclusive in the apostolic nature of the Holy Spirit. Cannistraci calls the Spirit of God an "Apostolic Spirit". (6) He says, "The entire apostolic movement will be permeated with the presence, power and activity of the Holy Spirit." (7)

Understanding the nature of co-operating with the Holy Spirit is basic to the apostolic culture. Cannistraci says it is impossible to understand the apostolic, apart from its relationship to the Holy Spirit. Paul's rhetoric confirms this point. (8)

When Paul ended his second letter to the Corinthians by saying, "The fellowship of the Holy Spirit, be with you all" (2 Corinthians 13:14), he underscored the depth and breadth of Spirit-filled leadership and living. The Greek word for "fellowship" is koinonia, meaning

> **Being and doing are mutually inclusive in the apostolic nature of the Holy Spirit.**

intercourse, partnership and participation. The first meaning, intercourse, reflects the intimate nature of our relationship with the Holy Spirit.

In *The Holy Spirit My Senior Partner*, Paul Yonggi Cho calls the Holy Spirit the "senior partner" of his daily life. (9) He believes that, without fervent and daily fellowship with the Holy Spirit, believers become cold and worship becomes mechanical. Is it possible that perfunctory religious activities in much of Christendom today are for lack of a Spirit-saturated life?

Jesus, determined to spare his disciples from the trappings of powerless religion, exhorted them to keep asking the Father for more of the Spirit (Luke 11:13). He told them that the Holy Spirit would teach them everything and guide them everywhere (John 14:26; 16:13). No wonder He commanded them to not leave town without it (Luke 24:49).

Cannistraci says apostles and apostolic leadership have a uniquely dependent relationship on the Holy Spirit. (10) It is precisely this dependence that helps shape a Spirit-filled culture, where partnering with his presence everywhere is as normal as breathing.

This second meaning of koinonia, "partnership" and "participation", is the natural by-product of a Spirit-filled life. When you walk with someone as closely as the apostles and believers walked with the Holy Spirit, discerning where you should or shouldn't go can be as clear as distinguishing between a green light and a red light. Language like, "Having been forbidden by the Holy Spirit to speak the Word in Asia" and "They were trying to go into Bithynia, and the Spirit of Jesus did not permit them" (Acts 16:6–7) highlights two significant implications.

> **Is it possible that perfunctory religious activities in much of Christendom today are for lack of a Spirit-saturated life?**

Firstly, since the Holy Spirit is, as Yonggi Cho says, "the senior partner", any ministry action taken must be a co-operative between God and people. Commenting on how the Holy Spirit initiated Paul's first missionary journey, Cho states, "Here the Holy Spirit emphasised that the ambassador extraordinary and plenipotentiary (with full powers) is neither a denomination nor any human person, but the Holy Spirit Himself." (11)

The fact that they were ministering to the Lord and fasting emphasises the priority of seeking Him with no other agenda than the relationship. Rather than seeking a blessing for their plans, they were seeking the One who blesses. This leads to a second proposition: strategies and plans must be yielded to the leadership of the Holy Spirit. Cho notes that many believers have already "monopolised the leadership of their lives", i.e. they have determined their own plans and are only looking for the Holy Spirit to bless their well-organised blueprints. (12)

Which qualities are most conducive to living a Spirit-saturated life, and how can leaders avoid the trap of being led more by their watertight strategies than by God?

When the 12 apostles announced to the entire congregation their intention to remain devoted "to prayer and to the ministry of the Word" (Acts 6:4), they revealed a few essentials for being Spirit-saturated and bringing the Kingdom: personal experience, revelation and demonstration. For the apostles, prayer was about spending exclusive time encountering his presence. Jesus was their model for prayer, which meant being in the Father's presence and then doing what they saw the Father doing (John 5:19).

Strategies and plans must be yielded to the leadership of the Holy Spirit.

Equally significantly, Jesus made it clear that the purpose of the Word was to reveal Him (John 5:39). An apostolic approach to the Word of God was more than just memorising letters on parchments, and then teaching and preaching. Paul said, "My message and my preaching were not in persuasive words ... but in demonstration of the Spirit and of power" (1 Corinthians 2:4).

After Peter and John's first arrest, the entire congregation prayed "with one accord", asking for boldness to speak the Word, with encounters and demonstrations following (Acts 4:24–30). Evangelist and author Mario Murillo describes it as asking for more of self to be buried in new waves of Holy Spirit power. (13)

Bill Johnson made a sobering point when he wrote, "Any revelation from God's Word that does not lead us to an encounter with God only serves to make us more religious." (14) For him, prayer and the ministry of the Word are not just liturgical exercises, but conduits for encountering his presence and demonstrating his Kingdom.

Firstly, prayer is more than just a perfunctory commitment to a daily spiritual exercise. Brother Lawrence, author of *Practicing the Presence of God,* called prayer "nothing else but a sense of God's presence." (15) Often referred to as the apostle of prayer, E.M. Bounds captured the heart of both prayer and the apostolic when he wrote, "Prayer puts God in full force in the world. To a prayerful man God is present in realised force." (16)

Discipline for the purpose of prayer is important, with regard to harnessing self from a host of distractions, but it's the engaging of God's presence that prayer is intended for. To discipline oneself for prayer without encountering God can be a dangerous proposition. Bill Johnson, who calls intimacy the "main purpose of prayer", (17) argues that the lack of encountering God will lead to misunderstanding the Word. (18)

Jesus told the Sadducees, who were challenging Him on the validity of the resurrection, that their understanding was wrong because they did not "know" the Scriptures, nor the power of God (Matthew 22:29, NLT). The word "know", or knowing, means much more than just the accumulation of information. If that were not the case, then Jesus would not have corrected the Sadducees, who possessed lots of information about God. The Greek word that Jesus used for knowing God is eido, meaning to see, to experience. Prayer, in essence, is about seeing or experiencing God. It is within this experiential context that real understanding of the Word (the Bible) occurs.

> **Any revelation from God's Word that does not lead us to an encounter with God only serves to make us more religious.**

In fact, in most human relationships, experience precedes understanding. For example, let's say I have just received a letter from a life-long friend who moved away a year ago. During my lunch break, I read the lengthy letter. It is a journey down memory lane. The letter is full of our many experiences together. One minute I am laughing and the next minute I am in tears. In other words, I am experiencing real emotions from the meaning of what is written.

Suddenly, I notice the time, and I hurry back to my office. In the rush, I accidentally leave the letter behind in the cafeteria. A complete stranger sees the letter, picks it up and begins to read it. He understands the words, but he does not understand the meaning of the stories; nor does he experience any of the emotion. Why? Simply because he does not know my friend or me; he does not have the relationship that gives meaning and power to what he is reading.

This in no way suggests that our personal experiences in prayer are more important than the Bible; it simply highlights the primacy of encountering Him through prayer, which acts as a catalyst for understanding and releasing the power of the Word. In God, they are mutually inclusive. E.M. Bounds called the Word and prayer the greatest essentials for a Spirit-filled life. (19) One of my best friends, Bob Perry, a prayer General in the Body of Christ, attributed his 11 years of missionary success in Latvia to the invincibility of "prayer-saturated Word".

In most human relationships, experience precedes understanding.

Secondly, the "ministry of the Word" is about the "Word" being materialised. When John wrote, "And the Word became flesh, and dwelt among us," he was describing the incarnation of the Word of God through the life and ministry of Jesus (John 1:14).

John also applied incarnation to every believer when he wrote "Little children, let us not love with word or with tongue, but in deed and truth" (1 John 3:18).

Just as a product without a guarantee is not good business, or a promise without action is not good government, the message without the miraculous is not the "ministry of the Word". The writer of Hebrews supported this experiential approach to the ministry of the Word when he wrote, "For the Word of God is living and active" (Hebrews 4:12).

The message without the miraculous is not the "ministry of the Word.

The Greek word for "ministry" is diakonia, meaning service. It's a revelation and demonstration of what is written. This is the primary role of the Holy Spirit, who is called the "Spirit of truth" (John 14:17).

Jesus said, "He will glorify Me, for He will take of Mine and will disclose it to you" (John 16:14). The word "glorify" is translated from the Greek word doxazo. It means to make conspicuous divine character and attributes. This is the essence of what it means to be "doers of the Word, and not merely hearers who delude themselves" (James 1:22).

The very nature of disclosure or revelation acts as a catalyst for experience and/or demonstration. If that were not so, then simple information like "Jesus is the

130

Saviour" could save anyone who heard it. In other words, it takes revelation, or the revealing of that truth before faith can make it a reality in the human heart. According to Jesus, without the Holy Spirit, revelation is not possible. Paul said, "For to us God revealed them through the Spirit; for the Spirit searches all things, even the depths of God" (1 Corinthians 2:10). Both the revelation and the demonstration are part of what it means to exercise the "ministry of the Word". Few leaders would disagree with the notion that it is wrong to say to someone, "Go in peace, be warmed and be filled" and then make no effort to help them with what they need (James 2:16).

However, many leaders today preach and teach a Gospel message that's designed to save, deliver and heal, with very little of those benefits following. In fact, Paul told the Corinthians that, when he returned to Corinth, he would expose the arrogance of those who taught in word only (1 Corinthians 4:19-20).

Bill Johnson says that proving the will of God means not only declaring that the Kingdom is at hand, but also demonstrating its effects. (20) Herein lies one of the most significant characteristics of Spirit-filled leadership and any developing apostolic leadership culture: having ongoing signs, wonders and miracles in and through the Body of Christ. A supernatural lifestyle is essential to the ministry of apostles and the subsequent culture they shape.

Supernatural Living

Regardless of the ignorance, criticism and/or fears surrounding the role of the Holy Spirit and the supernatural in the Church, the volume of signs, wonders and miracles throughout the Body of Christ is rising. Cannistraci calls the demonstration of true supernatural power one of the most exciting features of the ministry of the apostle and the entire apostolic movement. (21)

The confirming power of the Holy Spirit has been a hallmark characteristic of apostolic ministry since the days of the early disciples. There has seldom been a time, throughout 31 years of full-time Christian ministry, that Connie and I have not been acutely aware of the interventions and demonstrations

> **The confirming power of the Holy Spirit has been a hallmark characteristic of apostolic ministry since the days of the early disciples.**

131

of the Holy Spirit. From the straightening of vertebras misshapen by scoliosis to the healing of cancers and HIV, the presence and power of the Holy Spirit has continually confirmed the Word preached.

From angelic protection to the supernatural multiplication of McDonald's hamburgers, we have seen how comprehensive life with the Spirit can be. Whether it was money materialising out of thin air, as experienced by some college students from His People Church in Durban, South Africa, or literally getting water out of the rock, as a farmer did in the city of George, South Africa, the Holy Spirit's activity has never ceased to amaze us.

When Dr Mel Siff, a professor at the University of the Witwatersrand and hard-core agnostic, walked into my Johannesburg office, I was given a stark reminder of Holy Spirit power and supernatural living. Honestly, I was a bit intimidated by this encyclopaedia on legs. Not that I was a complete apologetic lightweight, but he was Nobel Prize calibre. In fact, for several hours prior to Dr. Siff stepping into my office, I was on the phone soliciting intellectual ammunition from my smarter friends.

Once he'd settled in his chair across from me at my desk, he proceeded to tell me about a strange experience he'd had while lecturing at a conference in Denver, Colorado. While I was pondering on how to respond to this paragon of brilliance, hoping for something semi-impressive, the Holy Spirit told me to ask him whether I could pray for him. That didn't sound all too brilliant, but I knew how to do that. He agreed, so I moved around the desk to where he was seated. As soon as I laid my hand on him, he was knocked to the floor.

For the next 20 minutes, all I did was pray in the Holy Spirit, while he cried out to God, weeping, confessing and repenting. By the time he got off the floor, he was born again and filled with the Holy Spirit. He became a faithful member of His People congregation in Johannesburg. Dr Siff got changed by the supernatural power of God, and not by any persuasive words on my part.

At God Adventure church in East London, South Africa, veteran church planters Nigel and Debbie Desmond are experiencing what happens "when God colours outside the lines." (22) Their Church has become a wellspring of signs, wonders and miracles. Refusing to be ashamed of anything the Holy Spirit chooses to do, they are cultivating a Kingdom atmosphere that is serving the city and the broader Body of Christ.

Recently, a tour group from France, who'd heard about what God was doing through this church, spent a week there being powerfully impacted by the move of the Holy Spirit. Although the role of the Holy Spirit is far greater than any single gift, miracle or manifestation, Paul's statement to the Corinthians about the evidence of "true" apostolic leadership including signs, wonders and miracles (2 Corinthians 12:12) provides a litmus test for all subsequent apostles.

Paul told the Roman Christians that it was "in the power of signs and wonders, in the power of the Spirit" that he "fully preached the gospel of Christ" (Romans 15:19). Today, the Holy Spirit's creative ability to save, deliver and heal has extended far beyond crusade evangelists in deep, dark Africa.

> **Today, the Holy Spirit's creative ability to save, deliver and heal has extended far beyond crusade evangelists in deep, dark Africa.**

Believers throughout the Body of Christ are being used in powerful ways. From the healing rooms of the Bethel Church in Redding, California to congregations all across America, testimonies of creative miracles and healings are abounding. To this day, one of the greatest miracles that Connie and I have ever been a part of was when God gave Wesley Steelburg a brand new heart at the Maranatha World Leadership Conference in Tulsa, Oklahoma.

Wesley, whose father had been the general superintendent of the Assemblies of God, was one of the most loved pastors in America. He was told by his doctors that he only had a few weeks to live. He was brought to the conference auditorium in a wheelchair, with a heart so damaged that he was having to take more nitro-glycerine to stay alive than any other person in history.

After Wesley had been honoured by my apostolic leader, Bob Weiner (Wesley was one of Bob's spiritual fathers), many leaders were called onto the platform to pray for him. Bob had just been handed a note stating, "Wesley is having a heart attack right now." We experienced a literal "on earth as it is in heaven" moment. The Holy Spirit put a new heart in Wesley's chest. His doctor at Eisenhower Medical said, "This is a modern-day miracle."

Sometime after this amazing, creative miracle, his wife commented that it was like being married to a teenager. She was struggling to keep up with him!

From extensive revival meetings held in East London, South Africa by Rev. Rodney Howard Brown to individual believers throughout the Body of Christ in South Africa, Holy Spirit power is being increasingly manifested. The invasion of God into impossible situations comes through a people who have received power from on high and have learnt to release it into the circumstances of life.

A sustained outpouring of signs, wonders and miracles is endemic to an apostolic leadership culture. Jesus made it clear that it is evidence of the Kingdom coming. The entire tone of Acts 2 reflects the transition of divine enablement from an Old Testament model of God and the Law through a few, to a relational framework of Jesus, grace and the Holy Spirit through an entire people.

> **A sustained outpouring of signs, wonders and miracles is endemic to an apostolic leadership culture.**

It is both experiential and transformational. As Bill Johnson notes, "The mission of heaven is to infiltrate earth with its realities." (23) While commenting on the real influence of spiritual leadership, Oswald Sanders noted that it was not by the power of personality alone, but by that "personality irradiated, interpenetrated, and empowered by the Holy Spirit". (24)

In his admonishment of the Corinthians, Paul expressed these sentiments and set a benchmark for recognising the Kingdom. He said, "For the Kingdom of God does not consist in words but in power" (1 Corinthian 4:20). As previously stated, so strong was Paul's position, that he ignored impressive rhetoric, and measured the authenticity of Corinthian leadership by the evidence of change and transformation. Part of that transformation is the long-term health and growth of leaders and their churches.

When Paul reminded the Galatians that they would reap in due season, if they did not grow weary (Galatians 6:9), he was referring to their wellbeing over an extended period of time. In the preceding verse, Paul said, "But the one who sows to the Spirit will from the Spirit reap eternal life" (Galatians 6:8). In other words, he placed their long-term welfare squarely in the context of their relationship with the Holy Spirit.

So, equally noteworthy among the roles and functions of the Holy Spirit is the renewal and longevity of his leaders. Paul's last recorded words to Timothy were, "I have finished the course, I have kept the faith" (2 Timothy 4:7). This Greek word for "faith" is pistis, meaning a term indicative of the means of appropriating what God in Christ has for man. Paul's testimony here relates to the sustainability of his life and leadership in God.

The sustainability and growth of an apostolic culture requires personal renewal that is spiritual, intellectual, emotional and physical. For Paul, this was also the domain of the Holy Spirit. He said to Titus, "He saved us ... by the washing of regeneration and renewing by the Holy Spirit" (Titus 3:5). The two primary Hebrew words for "renew" denote an experience that is both a cutting off and a building up.

> **The sustainability and growth of an apostolic culture requires personal renewal that is spiritual, intellectual, emotional and physical.**

After Jesus was baptised and filled with the Holy Spirit, He was led by the Spirit into the wilderness. The Holy Spirit's renewal process includes both removal and regeneration. One of the most dynamic examples of personal renewal is where Scripture refers to the fact that "your youth is renewed like the eagle" (Psalm 103:5). Some common and insightful understanding surrounding an eagle's renewal underscores this dual process.

Known as the moulting process, an eagle will go through a renewal season (lasting up to five months) that is both a death and a resurrection. From the age of 30 to 40, the claws and beak of an eagle are in disrepair and the feathers cumbersome. Calcium deposits cause brittleness in its beak, and its talons are weakened.

If it is able to secure a place high up, in its nest or a small cave, it can go through this renewal process in safety. It will pluck out its own talons and break its beak, after which they are replaced by new ones. During this time, the feathers will also be completely renewed. This renewal can add another 30 years to the life of an eagle.

This imagery of renewal for the eagle parallels the manner of renewal for leaders in an apostolic leadership culture. It includes focused timeout, vulnerability, pain, patience and new growth. Even more telling is the safe environment of the nest or cave. That safe place for a leader is to stay saturated with the Holy Spirit, and situated in apostolically based familial relationships.

It is an environment characterised by vulnerability, trust and change. Dallas Willard noted the supernatural nature of this Spirit encounter when he said, "The resources extend way beyond the human." (25) Supernatural encounters, whether confirming the Word preached, or transforming the preacher of the Word, are an ever-present quality among true apostolic ministries.

That safe place for a leader is to stay saturated with the Holy Spirit, and situated in apostolically based familial relationships.

This feature is, however, not without its critics. One criticism launched against believers who pursue supernatural encounters, whether for personal renewal or ministry-related purposes, is the 'bless me club' syndrome. Christians pressing in for more impartation or anointing are viewed by some as naive, at best, or idolatrous, at worst.

The problem with this view is that it neglects the model of Scripture, the supernatural nature of man and the mandate for reaching a lost world. Jesus and his disciples sought fresh encounters with the Holy Spirit, and then poured it out in the form of revival and transformation, while Paul told the Corinthians, "Desire earnestly spiritual gifts, but especially that you may prophesy" (1 Corinthians 14:1).

There is always the likelihood that some Christians (like Peter, James and John on the Mount of Transfiguration) will try and camp out around a sensational personal experience, but that does not diminish the priority of the Holy Spirit in releasing power through the Church for personal renewal, salvation, deliverance, healing and social transformation.

Bill Johnson noted, "Multi-generational revival, along with societal transformation (the Kingdom coming on earth as it is in heaven), are at the top of God's agenda." (26) Apostolic leaders are fathers who create Kingdom environments where God's people encounter God and bring a lost world into a God encounter.

Creating these Kingdom environments requires greater intentionality between apostolic leaders and the next generation of holy firebrands. Which attitudes and actions are most critical for fostering ongoing renewal? What hinders and what helps leaders to stay the course and keep the faith? What is the role of rest and renewal in leadership longevity?

Rest and Renewal

One of the biggest challenges for the Western mind is to hold diverse ideas, focuses and functions in healthy tension. In his book *The Leadership Challenge in Africa* Gerhard van Rensburg noted that Western societies are more influenced by the "isolated self" and the "fragmentation of life", as differentiated from holistic views and complementary orientations. (27) This has resulted in the mastering of parts, at the expense of whole systems, relationships and communities.

The human tendency to engage in behaviour, actions and relationships without considering processes, environments or other reciprocating variables, has led to everything from muscle tears and dysfunctional relationships to disasters in civil government. When runners don't stretch, family members don't communicate and voters don't investigate beyond populist rhetoric, breakdown is unavoidable.

> **One of the biggest challenges for the Western mind is to hold diverse ideas, focuses and functions in healthy tension.**

This is equally true for our quest to understand and implement the process of rest and renewal. Is this process as simple as hitting the pause button one day a week? Does honouring the principle of the Hebrew Sabbath automatically translate into a re-energised body and soul? Or is rest and renewal a more robust process of interacting elements? What does a Biblical process of rest look like and how does it benefit individuals and organisations?

The Sabbath

Observing the Sabbath rest is one of the oldest traditions in the world. Dating back as far as the Biblical record of creation (where God rested from his work of creation and blessed the seventh day), the Sabbath day was ratified into Jewish law and culture, becoming a standard bearer in man's relationship to God and society.

137

Ostensibly, the Sabbath represented a fixed point in time for spiritual reflection, rest and renewal, while, as a principle, a day of rest continues to occupy the calendars of most contemporary societies. Is the day of rest merely a moment of obedience; a specific time to focus on nothing but God? Is it just common sense applied to human physiology? Or is there more to it? What is this "remarkable truth hidden in the strange institution of the Sabbath", as Ray Stedman calls it? (28)

According to Matthew Henry, God began the "Sabbath Rest" by reflecting on all that He had made. He says, "Having given us the power of reflection, He expects us to use that power, see our way and think of it." (29) In other words, it's about approaching the whole of life from the centrality of his finished work.

It combines the unshakable foundation of God's finished work with the blend and balances of various life priorities.

Herein lie two of the most significant reminders from the Sabbath day: the centrality of God's perfect provision and the complementarities of life. It combines the unshakable foundation of God's finished work with the blend and balances of various life priorities.

In an article by Mind Tools (a leadership and management service provider), a life-balancing tool called The Wheel of Life is explained. They note that when the lion's share of a person's energy is focused on a single project or a job description, it's all too easy to find oneself off balance, and not pay enough attention to other important areas of life. (30)

In their book The Truth about Burnout Christina Maslach and Michael Leiter note that the lack of time and energy given to other human values in the organisational environment is a major contributor to worker burnout. (31)

What is true for organisations is equally true for individuals. Maintaining health and productivity over a sustained period of time will mean blending all the significant areas of our human design. It will mean restraining the potential hubris of single passions, functions or experiences by prioritising other spiritual, emotional, physical and social needs. Put another way, it's about idolatry-proofing the human soul!

138

Arresting Idolatry

One of the primary benefits of the Sabbath rest is to protect humankind from the trappings of idolatry. In *No God but God*, Richard Keyes says that an idol is something in creation that we inflate beyond its purpose and function. (32) It is any object that replaces the primacy of God in an individual's life and undermines

> **It's about idolatry-proofing the human soul!**

the blend and balances of reciprocating life functions. For example, a husband's passion for financial security can quickly morph into an idol that undermines both his spiritual and relational priorities. Or a pastor's strategic focus on church growth can easily undermine the very community it's been created to reach and serve.

Contrary to popular belief, God's moment of rest on the seventh day represented more than just a respite in activity. Scripture says that God rested from the specific project of creation, but He didn't cease from all activity. In other words, God's "rest" connected his creation to other priorities. It allowed Him to turn his attention to specific relationships that his finished work was designed to serve, Man.

As Jesus said, "The Sabbath was made for man, and not man for the Sabbath." (Mark 2:27). Rest represented both the centrality of God as life-giver and the necessity of diverse life functions and

> **Idolatry undermines both vertical and horizontal priorities.**

needs. Idolatry undermines both vertical and horizontal priorities. A disregard for God in someone's life can often lead to neglect of their personal health, relationships or responsibilities. This neglect is commonly found in the arenas of physical, mental and emotional needs.

Paul's comment to Timothy that "bodily discipline is only of little profit" (1 Timothy 4:8) was an issue of comparison to eternal realities, and not a treatise on the irrelevance of physical needs. He actually placed a premium on bodily discipline by reminding the Corinthians to glorify God in their bodies.

Interestingly, reference to the physiology of the human body is the most common metaphorical rhetoric used in Scripture. David captured the value of our human anatomy when he wrote, "You formed my inward parts; you wove me in my mother's womb" (Psalm 139:13). When Jesus said, "Come away by yourselves to a secluded place and rest a while" (Mark 6:31), He was underscoring the priority of a leader's physical rest.

According to studies on the brain, a lack of rest, which leads to significant sleep deprivation, causes the neurons in the brain to malfunction. According to Sarah Ledoux in *The Effects of Sleep Deprivation on Brain and Behavior* the frontal lobe is the most important section of the brain with relation to sleep deprivation. Its functions are associated with speech, as well as novel and creative thinking. She says that sleep-deprived people do not have the speed or creative abilities to cope with making quick, but logical decisions; nor do they have the ability to implement them. (33)

Studies have demonstrated that a lack of sleep impairs one's ability to simultaneously focus on several different related tasks, reducing the speed, as well as the efficiency of one's actions. Ledoux says that sleep-deprived people tend to be unimaginative and repetitive in their communication. If this is true, how much failure in leadership can be traced back to a lack of rest and sleep deprivation?

The donkeys taught the atheists a lesson in practical theology.

The French found out the hard way after the French Revolution. The government moved the seven-day work week to a ten-day cycle. In a short span of time, the horses and mules began to die out at an alarming rate. Upon investigation, scientists determined that the seven-day principle was necessary for health and long life. Someone said, "The donkeys taught the atheists a lesson in practical theology." (34)

Of course, the best teachers to address the need and function of "rest" are the Holy Spirit and Scripture. Among the many Biblical insights pertaining to "rest" is David's approach in the Book of Psalms.

A Model from David

A very insightful progression relating to rest and renewal is found in Psalm 37. Firstly, in Psalm 37:8, David said, "Cease from anger and forsake wrath; Do not fret; it leads only to evildoing." How many times have we attempted to follow that command? Yet, how many times have we failed miserably? Of course, ceasing from fear or anger, without understanding and accessing the source, is like trying to get out of debt by using more credit cards.

One verse earlier, David said, "Rest in the Lord." So, to "rest in the Lord" becomes the basis for overcoming anger and fear. In other words, the "rest" has renewed and strengthened the soul's capacity to overcome in very difficult circumstances. But how do we "rest in the Lord"? If renewal and strength only takes place in the place of "rest", how do we get there?

We actually have a process of rest and renewal that goes back to verses 3–5. The progression is: "Trust in the Lord" (v. 3); "Delight yourself in the Lord" (v. 4); "Commit your ways to the Lord" (v. 5); and then "Rest in the Lord" (v.7).

The first time David uses this Hebrew word for trust (batach) is in Psalm 4:4–5. It is in the context of "Meditate in your heart upon your bed, and be still ... trust in the Lord." It is used less precipitately than the other Hebrew word for trust (chasah) and is, therefore, more childlike. It's the capacity of the heart to take God at his Word, regardless of anything contrary. This leads to delighting in the Lord.

This word delight means to make merry. It also speaks of jesting with God; having fun with Him. This is similar to being with your best friend where you are free to be yourself. Jesus was constantly celebrating and having fun. Why else would children be so attracted to Him? Only from this place can we truly commit our ways to the Lord. To commit means to push or roll it over onto the Lord.

> **Jesus was constantly celebrating and having fun.**

Have you ever tried to push something over and didn't have the strength or leverage, so it just rolled back towards you? The word commit evokes the same kind of imagery. The strength to commit something to the Lord flows from delighting in Him. Just keep delighting in Him until there is the strength to roll it over.

This is the place from where real rest and renewal comes. Although rest and renewal is anything but formulaic, the principles and processes of the "Sabbath rest" can easily be understood, exercised and enjoyed. God, who is well aware of the intricacies of our design, has provided some restorative pauses in the relentless pace of our contemporary schedules. Whether it means idolatry-proofing the human heart, or simply tanking up the spirit, soul and body for the journey ahead, hitting the refresh button on both the centrality of God as the only life-giver and the complementary nature of diverse life functions should be a non-negotiable part of every believer's life.

Conclusion

In his book *The Last Great Anointing* Morris Cerullo describes a world-changing anointing that he sees coming to and through the Body of Christ. This world-renowned apostle-prophet describes a vision that the Lord gave him over 50 years ago in Lima, Peru. The vision related to a season in the future when unprecedented anointing and authority would be released worldwide through men and women of God.

He heard the Lord say audibly, "What I do on the earth will be entirely without human direction, so that no man can put his name on it. This will not be the work of man, but of the Holy Spirit." Meaning, the Holy Spirit will be as prominent and powerful among the people as in the days of the early apostles, or, as Dr Cho describes it, "The Holy Spirit My Senior Partner".

As we fast-forward into our 21st century global context, the realisation of that divine declaration is upon us. In spite of the ongoing trauma of economic instability, abject poverty, global terrorism, political turmoil, moral degeneration and natural disasters, the nations of the earth are being visited by an apostolic people who are walking in new dimensions of Holy Spirit revelation and demonstration.

Rather than being a movement organised and led by a few spiritual superstars, it is Body-wide. Instead of it being personality focused, it is Holy Spirit focused. In other words, the centrality of intimacy with God's presence, coupled with the revelation and demonstration of his Word, is once again the basis for apostolic authority and leadership. This Spirit-saturated life and ministry creates a leadership culture where signs, wonders and miracles are a normal occurrence;

Rather than being a movement organised and led by a few spiritual superstars, it is Body-wide.

and where leaders experience the rest and renewal necessary for continued growth, and for ending strong.

Being centred on the Holy Spirit or his presence is one of the best ways to idolatry-proof the human soul. Man's proclivity towards Babel-building can be avoided by paying greater attention to understanding and experiencing the nature of the Holy Spirit.

An apostolic leadership culture is an environment suitable for bringing the Kingdom of God "on earth as it is in heaven", and Spirit-filled enablement is heaven's provision towards that end. Therefore, among the throngs of people being mobilised to bring sustainable transformation, are believers who will experience and demonstrate the nature of God in the power of the Holy Spirit.

Discussion Questions

6.1 How would you describe the role of the Holy Spirit?

6.2 Explain how you usually experience the Holy Spirit.

6.3 What Bible verses do you use when referring to the Holy Spirit?

6.4 What are you specifically doing in order to grow in your relationship with the Holy Spirit?

6.5 Describe any supernatural encounters/experiences you've had.

6.6 How would you describe being at rest in the Lord?

6.7 What is the purpose of the Sabbath? Explain how it affects your life.

6.8 Have you experienced "burnout" as a leader, and what have you done to recover from its effects, and prevent it from happening again?

CHAPTER SEVEN

Conclusion

An apostolic leadership culture is simply an environment where the beliefs, values and behaviour of heaven, as represented and modelled by apostles and apostolic teams, become characteristic of a community of people who are being activated to bring sustainable change and transformation to their communities and cities. It is about bringing the Kingdom of God "on earth as it is in heaven".

In order to develop this Kingdom culture, leaders throughout the Body of Christ need an apostolic understanding of both the Kingdom message and the messenger of the Church. The wine of God's redemptive message and the wineskin of Man's efforts need appropriate definition and congruency.

In *The Problem of Wineskins: Church Structure in a Technological Age*, Howard Snyder makes a compelling argument for the necessity of "new wineskins". He says that when the Gospel and the power of God touch human culture, "wineskins" are formed. (I) In other words, structures and the way of doing things, which are influenced by the local culture, are developed for the purpose of representing and serving the nature of God's message and power.

> **The wine of God's redemptive message and the wineskin of Man's efforts need appropriate definition and congruency.**

Wineskins are simply the way of His Church in culture. Unfortunately, the way of His Church has often fallen into the trap of its Jewish predecessor. Rather

145

> **Rather than adjusting to the newness of God in every new generation or culture, the Church became a defender of outdated traditions and structures.**

than adjusting to the newness of God in every new generation or culture, the Church became a defender of outdated traditions and structures. When Jesus was being challenged by the Pharisees for allowing his disciples to "transgress the traditions of the elders", He retorted, "They put new wine into fresh wineskins, and both are preserved" (Matthew 9:17).

Jesus threw down the proverbial gauntlet against the rigid parochialism that characterised the Judaism of his day. Snyder argues for an understanding of the Church that reflects both the newness of God and its relevance in society. He goes on to say, "When the Bible says 'church' it does not normally mean an invisible, ethereal reality divorced from space and time any more than it means an institutional organisation." (2)

He refers to the Church as a "communal form of the Kingdom of God in the present age" and describes the Kingdom as God's redeeming lordship successfully winning over the hearts of men, their lives and the whole of creation. (3) As argued in this book, and specifically in Chapter One, this is an apostolic approach to the mandate of the Church.

The benchmark for apostolic leadership and ministry is to bring the Kingdom "on earth as it is in heaven". As George Ladd said, the Kingdom of God is the "realisation of God's perfect reign in all the universe". (4) Whatever we can imagine in heaven, is God's intention for planet earth.

> **Whatever we can imagine in heaven, is God's intention for planet earth.**

Jesus' life and ministry is the model for apostolic leaders, as well as his redeemed communities.

Everything from salvation, deliverance and healing to the transformation of civil society is found within the apostolic mandate. Equally true, the continued role of the apostle is paramount to the advancement of the Kingdom. The unique contribution of apostles and apostolic leaders was a common feature in how the Gospel impacted and influenced first-century Mediterranean culture.

A first-century understanding of an apostle left little room for confusion regarding its extensive nature. Just as Roman apostles were called to represent the emperor and replicate Rome in conquered territories, Kingdom apostles are called and anointed to replicate heaven on earth.

From the evidence of Scripture and Church history, apostles: a) represent God; b) are a gift to the entire Body of Christ; c) are relationally grounded; d) are prolific activators of diverse leaders and ministries; e) function in the power of signs, wonders and miracles; f) build apostolic teams; and g) develop creative and relevant strategies capable of cross-cultural ministry.

Even more significant, is an apostolic company and the subsequent Kingdom culture that grows from the influence of apostolic ministry. Cannistraci notes that God will not change the world through a handful of apostles, but through a vast company of apostolic people. (5) Among the most significant qualities necessary for developing this apostolic/Kingdom culture are suitable values.

> **Among the most significant qualities necessary for developing this apostolic/ Kingdom culture are suitable values.**

When Jesus declared, "Where your treasure is, there your heart will be also" (Matthew 6:21), He was connecting our treasures, or what we greatly value, with our core nature and drive. The Greek word used for "heart" is kardia, meaning the seat and centre of circulation, and therefore of human life. He identified the "heart" as a place of deep desire that generates our thoughts, attitudes, behaviour and actions.

Understanding the role that our "values organ" (the heart) plays in the drive and development of a Kingdom culture is critical. As noted by James O' Toole, leading by the pull of inspiring values is not just an option in a sea of equally valid leadership concepts and models; it is a must. (6) With the high visibility of universally pursued values and principles such as human dignity, personal responsibility, power-sharing, transparency, accountability, empowerment and others, the social psyche is becoming more resistant to the bottlenecks created by top-heavy leadership styles and practices. Values-based leadership is no longer an ideal, it is an essential.

For an apostolic leadership culture, identifying the right values, as well as their congruent attitudes, behaviour and actions, is paramount. If the culture is going to be a values-driven transformational environment, as argued in Chapter Two, then the values of knowing God and loving others will occupy the lion's share of intentionality. Growing in the knowledge of God experientially and loving people powerfully are not only the two Great Commandments, they are the currencies of heaven.

Paul told the Corinthians that there was a realm of love for God and for others that would not fail (1 Corinthians 13). To value and love another person with the same passion and impact of Jesus is nurtured within the principle and practice of honour. As Fawn Parish noted, "When we honour another person from the vantage point of heaven, literally seeing them through God's eyes, the degree of impact is determined by God's capacities rather than our own." (7)

Of course, the real motivator behind such Kingdom benevolence and power is found in knowing God and his goodness. I agree with Tozer's assertion that the whole outlook of mankind will be changed when we understand that we "dwell under a friendly sky". (8) It is this revelation of God's goodness that forms the basis for all that He accomplishes in and through an apostolic culture. It also lays the groundwork for the relational nature of the Kingdom and the Body of Christ.

> **Growing in the knowledge of God experientially and loving people powerfully are not only the two 'Great Commandments', they are the currencies of heaven.**

Erwin McManus says that the "apostolic ethos erupts out of the context of human relationships." (9) An apostolic leadership culture is typified by deep friendship with God and by Biblically based, familial relationships among believers. Jesus said the best evidence of a people belonging to Him was the calibre of love demonstrated among his own (John 13:35). A Pauline model for this kind of relationship is best understood in the framework of a family.

Interestingly, in all Paul's letters, he never used the term disciple or discipleship when describing Christians and their relationships. His rhetoric was thoroughly family-based, leaving little room for confusion as to the scope of how believers are meant to relate.

Equally relevant is the significance of fathering. Paul saw his apostolic ministry in the context of spiritual parenting. Fathering was viewed as essential for shaping a culture that was empowering for the next generation. Paul's relationship to young leaders like Timothy and Titus set a benchmark characterised by deep affection, sacrifice, honour and empowerment. As Bill Johnson said, "Apostles are first and foremost fathers," and the cultures they create are reflective of what fathers do best, which is facilitating development and growth. (10)

The familial quality of apostolic leadership was also described by Paul as being a "nursing mother" (1 Thessalonians 2:7). It represents the inexhaustible supply of motivation and sensitivity in the relationship. These familial-based relationships are multigenerational in orientation, i.e. the advancement of the Kingdom is realised through transference from one generation to another. The manner of partnership between young and old is critical for the passing on of inheritance, and its continued progress.

His rhetoric was thoroughly family-based, leaving little room for confusion as to the scope of how believers are meant to relate.

Paul's admonition to Timothy, "Entrust these to faithful men who will be able to teach others also" (2 Timothy 2:2), prioritises multigenerational transfer within the family of God. Implicit in Paul's command is the advancement of the Kingdom. One of the most valuable partnerships to emerge from these Biblically based familial relationships is mission-directed teams.

Productivity through relationships is best demonstrated when a diversity of leaders gather in unity towards a common mission or goal. Paul highlighted the extent of team effectiveness when he told the church in Ephesus that a partnership between apostles, prophets, evangelists, pastors and teachers would mature the saints to the point of demonstrating the fullness of Christ.

The apostolic mission of bringing the Kingdom into all walks of life is the rallying point for apostolic leaders and ministries. Within an apostolic leadership culture, the Kingdom mission supersedes any local church objectives and/or goals.

The Kingdom mission supersedes any local church objectives and/or goals.

149

The restoration of Jerusalem by Nehemiah and his team is a good example of the extensive impact of mission-directed teams. As seen by the example of Nehemiah, a team will agree on the mission and strategy before creating relevant structures and processes. Equally true, the number of changes within the environment will require significant flexibility among team members.

Similar to Nehemiah's success, the effectiveness of an apostolic team is predicated on: a) being God-initiated; b) having a common purpose; c) good communication; d) a continuous supply of diverse and complementary leaders; e) the currency of trust; f) a well-planned overall strategy; and g) flexibility and adaptability.

When developing an apostolic culture for effective transformation, team leaders should take their lead from principles and patterns revealed in Scripture. The "Genesis model" presented in Chapter Four highlights the value and primary purpose of team leadership. It is a matter of fundamental design, where productivity through diversity, personal development, focus, fit and enquiry results from partnering with God. This apostolic team dynamic has a unique ability to operate within culturally diverse environments, while releasing needed creativity and innovation.

Global or multicultural competencies, coupled with a steady supply of innovative strategies, structures and/or tools are a ubiquitous feature of the apostolic leadership culture. Although the basic message remained intact (declaring Christ and his reign in all spheres of life), the strategies and structures employed by Paul were adaptive and innovative.

> **The moment you think you've got the ministry all figured out, you're finished; in life and ministry.**

Whether in Antioch, Macedonia or Rome, Paul never ceased to bring the Gospel of the Kingdom, and he was continually adjusting to different cultural peculiarities. Rick Warren, writing the foreword for Erwin McManus's book *An Unstoppable Force* notes, "The moment you think you've got the ministry all figured out, you're finished; in life and ministry." (11)

Success in life and ministry, especially in the current global context, requires an ability to relate and create among diverse people groups. Our global village is

150

presenting more changes, challenges and opportunities; and at a faster pace than ever before. Therefore, a standardised or rigid approach to the Gospel ministry could mean the cessation of growth and impact. Erwin McManus describes the apostolic ethos as "fusing together a belief in the awesome nature of God and a stewardship of the God-given potential within every human being". (12)

The Apostle Paul's capacity to bring the Kingdom into a culturally diverse Mediterranean world, reflected his faith in a God who would do exceedingly abundantly beyond all he could ask or think (Ephesians 3:20), and demonstrated his ability to recognise no man according to the flesh (2 Corinthians 5:16). His impact among the Gentile world in Asia and Europe, as well as him being used by God to write two-thirds of the New Testament, is evidence of this apostolic quality.

From the early church to the Reformation, to future-focused apostolic ministries of the 21st century, an apostolic model of multicultural competence and innovation has emerged. According to McCall and Hollenbeck, the development of global competence takes place when our identities are assaulted by the crossing of cultural lines. Major differences will often provoke us to ask questions about ourselves and others, which can lead to greater self-awareness and change. (13)

There are cultural peculiarities, such as African Ubuntu, which assist the development of global capacity. Ubuntu is more effective in placing the identity, value and contribution of an individual within the interests of the community. As noted by Augustine Shutte, it encompasses the blend of integration and differentiation which makes synthesis and change more prodigious.

Among the benefits that accompany this Ubuntu ethic are: a) identifying with individuals within the community; b) diverse and challenging experiences; c) self-awareness; d) servant-leadership; and e) flexibility and adaptation.

This leads to another quality specific to apostolic leadership: global alliances and networking. Stewarding effective and sustainable transformation requires partnering across local church and denominational lines. As noted by Cannistraci, "Explosive advances are being made because people are connecting to increase the benefits for everyone. The trend is called 'networking' and many agree that it is the wave of the future because it is so effective." (14)

151

When the Body of Christ moves from the emergence of apostles to the convergence of apostolic ministries, the growth and transformation will be exponential. This has been witnessed in networks such as the Revival Alliance, Acts Twenty-Nine and the Transformation Movement. Of course, a common attribute found in these networks within this new apostolic season, is a greater understanding and reliance on the role of the Holy Spirit.

A relationship with the Holy Spirit is a non-negotiable quality for bringing powerful and sustainable transformation. As Bill Johnson says, the Holy Spirit is our "greatest gift". Regeneration and renewal is only made possible by the presence and power of the Holy Spirit (Titus 3:5). From a deeply intimate relationship with the Holy Spirit to the demonstration of signs, wonders and miracles, apostles and apostolic leaders today are modelling what the early church experienced in the Book of Acts.

> **When the Body of Christ moves from the emergence of apostles to the convergence of apostolic ministries, the growth and transformation will be exponential.**

As with the first apostles, the most life-changing and culture-shaping experiences come from within a leadership environment that is more conducive to the presence, direction and actions of the Holy Spirit. Instead of leaders being led by a watertight strategy, while hoping for the assistance of divine providence, apostles become Spirit-saturated through prayer and the ministry of the Word. They are led more by the time spent in God's presence than by their mission statements and job descriptions.

Similar to the model left by Jesus, an apostolic leadership culture is where people can see what the Father is doing and then respond accordingly. "Prayer and the ministry of the Word" are more than just perfunctory religious activities. They are time-intensive experiences with God, leading to the demonstration of the Word in power. The supernatural lifestyle is fundamental to the ministry of apostles and the cultures they shape. All over the world, displays of Kingdom power are evident. From the underground church in China to churches all across Africa and America, signs and wonders are increasing throughout the Body of Christ.

Equally significant to global revival, is the role of the Holy Spirit in bringing continued renewal to leaders. Bringing effective transformation will require the

152

continued health, strength and growth of God's people. Building for the long haul and finishing strong is what Paul meant when he told Timothy that he had finished the course and kept the faith (2 Timothy 4:7).

An apostolic leadership culture is where people and their relationships are more important than the work accomplished. To avoid the burnout and dropout of leaders and believers which is currently such a pandemic in the Body of Christ, apostles and apostolic leaders must create an atmosphere where knowing God and loving people are the primary motivators for ministry.

Applying the Sabbath rest and exposing idolatry are helpful remedies to the performance-orientation and religious rigidity currently damaging leaders and believers alike. The revelation and application of God's finished work, within the blend of diverse human priorities, can idolatry-proof and burnout-proof the human soul. The longevity needed to bring effective and sustainable transformation is realised within this Spirit-enabled lifestyle.

> **Apostles and apostolic leaders must create an atmosphere where knowing God and loving people are the primary motivators for ministry.**

Whether in Africa, Latin America, North America, Europe, Asia or Australia, our ability to bring the Kingdom of God "on earth as it is in heaven" will be decided by how we understand and implement the ministry of the apostolic. Developing an apostolic leadership culture is paramount to the task of global impact and transformation. It grows out of our value for God and people, and flourishes within familial-based relationships.

This apostolic culture comes loaded with amazing teams of diverse leaders who can relate cross-culturally and create new strategies. It is first and foremost a habitation for the Lord, where a supernatural lifestyle is most evident as the "kingdoms of this world become the Kingdoms of our Lord and Christ".

ADDENDUM A

Burnout and renewal in Christian organisations

In an article by Mind Tools (a leadership and management service provider), a life-balancing tool called The Wheel of Life was being promoted . The article stated that when the bulk of a leader's energy was focused on a single project or job description, it was all too easy to become off-balance; this means one is not paying enough attention to other important areas of the work environment and life.

In *The Truth about Burnout*, Christina Maslach and Michael Leiter noted that the lack of time and energy allocated to other human values in the organisational environment was a major contributor to leader burnout . Unfortunately, the Church as an organisation has not been immune to these imbalances.

According to the most recent studies, thousands of pastors and other church leaders leave the ministry and their local churches every year. Dr Richard J. Krejcir calls the job of Christian ministry a "dangerous occupation". An extensive study at the Francis A. Schaeffer Institute of Church Leadership Development found that 70 per cent of pastors were so "stressed out and burned out that they regularly consider leaving the ministry".

Between 35 and 40 per cent actually leave their churches within the first five years. The reasons and causes for leadership turnover in Christian organisations are many; some as innocuous as simple migration from one geographical location to another, and others as incendiary as relational dysfunctions and bitter conflicts. Among the many reasons for leader turnover in Christian organisations is the issue of burnout. Research distilled from Barna, Focus on the Family and Fuller Seminary revealed that about 1 500 pastors left the ministry every month because of "moral failure, spiritual burnout and contention in their churches".

When we look more closely, we find that one out of three pastors feel totally burned out within the first year alone, while one in three pastors see the ministry as hazardous to their families. Although senior pastors carry the significant brunt of ministry pressure, what is true for them seems to be true for other leaders within the church leadership structure.

The Extent of the Problem

If 1 500 senior pastors are leaving their churches every month, how many more associate leaders, lay leaders and congregants are doing the same? The revolving door for church leaders and members becomes glaringly apparent when we consider that more than 90 percent of mega-church growth is generated by Christians exiting other churches.

The number of leaders moving from one church to another is implicit in these numbers. Leaders at various levels of church organisations are leaving in mass numbers, and burnout is a significant contributing factor. Although the communication skills of the senior pastor are a major draw card for the mega-church, many Christians transferring from smaller congregations use the larger crowd as a buffer against co-dependent and dysfunctional relationships.

Addressing stress and burnout in the ministry, Rowland Croucher notes that even less competitive, Type-B Christians suffer burnout. He points out that these conscientious "people- helpers" are the most vulnerable. He refers to the problem as a "clash between expectations and reality". Croucher says that overexposure to the negative side of people's lives is problematic for these "people-helpers".

Burnout is the result of special stressors associated with unmanageable social and interpersonal pressures. In *Mad Church Disease, Overcoming the Burnout Epidemic*, Anne Jackson notes that burnout happens to Christian leaders worldwide, regardless of their age or position. She surveyed over 900 people serving in churches, and found that "almost every person who completed the questionnaire said the stress from ministry had affected them emotionally (most common were feelings of worthlessness, depression, anxiety, anger, or loneliness)".

In *Sabbaths and Sabbaticals: A Journey in Rest*, Susan Gaddis says the unattended stress that builds up within ministry relationships can destroy individuals, families and ministries. She highlights the role of the Sabbath and Sabbaticals as part of the renewal process. Benjamin Franklin's aphorism, "An ounce of prevention is better than a pound of cure," is very relevant for those seeking to stem the tide of burnout in Christian organisations.

To what degree is burnout affecting leaders in Christian organisations? How influential is the phenomenon of burnout in a leader's decision to abscond from their ministry responsibilities and relationships; and what is the role of rest and renewal as a preventive or curative process?

The Study

To better understand burnout as well as the role of rest and renewal in Christian organisations, a study of Christian leaders was conducted. The study looked at: 1) leaders who had left their Christian organisation; 2) the degree of burnout at the time of their departure; and 3) any actions taken for subsequent recovery and renewal. The leaders chosen for this study were serving in the same Christian organisation. For reasons of confidentiality and propriety, the organisation and the individuals involved will remain anonymous.

Over about a two-year period (with few exceptions), all these leaders had left the organisation. Most of the departures took place during a major restructuring of the organisation. Prior to the restructuring of the organisation, issues of abusive leadership practices, financial impropriety and unaccountable decision-making had surfaced, precipitating a major overhaul of the organisation's governance structure.

Prior to, during and after the organisational change, hundreds of leaders and dozens of churches left the organisation. Through the tireless efforts of new leadership, the organisation in question not only survived the mass exodus of leaders, but is beginning to thrive once again through a more Biblically based governance structure.

This study was in no way intended to disparage any individual leader or organisation. Its sole purpose was to identify the presence of burnout prior to and during the leader's departure, as well as the subsequent effects of any rest and renewal.

In their studies on burnout in organisations, Maslach and Leiter found compelling arguments that underscore the complicity of an organisation in the burnout of its employees. They define burnout as the "index of the dislocation between what people are and what they do in the organisational environment" . They say: "It represents the erosion in values, dignity, spirit, and will; an erosion of the human soul within a specific organisational context."

Backed by solid research, Maslach and Leiter assert that burnout is not a matter of personal weakness or poor attitude in individual leaders or employees. Rather, it is a problem of the social environment within a workplace, caused by major mismatches between the nature of the person doing a job and the nature of the job itself. The greater the mismatch is, the greater the potential for burnout. These authors cite six areas of mismatch in the work environment where burnout could emerge: workload, control, reward, community, fairness and values.

Their research formed the basis for assessing the potential burnout of the leaders in this study. During the initial phase of the study, more than 50 leaders who had formally served in diverse leadership roles in the organisation were contacted. This represents a sizable cross-section of the total number of leaders and churches that had left the organisation.

Once a positive response had been received from the individual leaders, the process began. Each participant was given two surveys to complete: the Maslach Burnout Inventory (MBI), which measures the degree of emotional exhaustion and depersonalisation; and the Ministry Burnout Assessment (MBA), which measures the six indices relative to burnout in the organisation (workload, control, reward, community, fairness and values).

Once the results had been tabulated, each participant received: 1) their scores (the degree of overall burnout, and burnout within each of the six indices); 2) an explanation of burnout within the organisational environment (according to the research of Christina Maslach and Michael Leiter); and 3) several texts pertaining to burnout, Sabbath rest and renewal.

After five days, each participant received a final questionnaire to identify any changes made related to burnout, rest and renewal; and to assess the overall learning experience from this exercise. Below are the results of the study.

The Results

Without exception, all participants measured moderate to high for overall burnout. In the six indices as identified by Maslach and Leiter, 86% of the leaders scored high in the breakdown of community, 66% scored high in the absence of fairness, 60% scored high in lack of control, 46% scored high in insufficient reward, 46% scored high in conflicting values and only 29% scored high in work overload. The fact that there was significant dissonance surrounding the issues of community, fairness and control highlights that there was a mismatch between participants' transformational leadership values and delivery of these values within the organisation.

In *The Leadership Challenge*, Richard Daft notes that transformational leaders develop followers into leaders, elevate the focus from lower-level physical needs to higher-level psychological and spiritual needs (self-esteem or self-actualisation), inspire leaders to go beyond self-interest, and paint a clear picture of a preferable state.

This leadership culture creates high expectancies. The expectancy theory, espoused by Victor Vroom, underscores the strong connection between increased effort and perceived benefits . Enormous personal sacrifice was expended in order to attain these transformational values; this was characteristic of many leaders within this Christian organisation. Herein lies a common organisational malady: disconnection between espoused values (individual and organisational) and actions. Often the degree of disappointment, disillusionment and burnout is proportional to the distance between expectations and personal experience. Further supporting this analysis is the organisational culture itself.

The organisation in question has strong clan (community), achievement (growth) and adhocracy (risk-taking) cultural characteristics. Among the organisation's core values are discipleship, leadership development, family and social responsibility. The outward focus of bringing social transformation is deeply rooted in a community ethic. Open and supportive relationships are highly valued.

As Daft says, "Leaders in the clan culture place a premium on fairness and reaching an agreement" . What was perceived as a "lack of fairness" by the majority of the participants was exacerbated by this strong familial culture. Maslach and

Leiter note that trust, openness and respect are key elements for fairness in organisations. They highlight open and honest communication as fostering fairness in the environment .

Good communication also makes decision-making more inclusive, which was lacking for many of the participants. Whether it was perception or reality, most leaders in this study felt disconnected from the type of open and honest discourse necessary to resolve many of the conflicts.

According to McKee, Johnson and Massimilian, the journey of renewal must begin with honest, thoughtful, and compassionate reflection and dialogue . For various reasons, this was not afforded the leaders being studied within their organisational environment. In addition, due to its strong missional focus, leadership actions or inactions that impede individual effort would invariably lead to frustration and conflict. For those involved in this study, leaving the organisation became the last measure for resolving the ongoing conflict and part of their process towards personal restoration and renewal.

Due to the nature of their long-standing relationships and a heart-felt commitment to the values and vision of the organisation, leaving proved to be emotionally traumatic for many of the leaders surveyed. Besides feeling shunned by an organisation that was not equipped to understand or address the real causes of their burnout, many of the leaders had to battle with the self-accusation of it must be my fault.

In a Christian culture where you are encouraged to continually examine your own heart, and to always believe the best of every person, excessive introspection and self-condemnation are common problems. Even the way that society views burnout argues for the fault of the individual.

Maslach and Leiter concur that the weakness of the individual is commonly viewed as the cause of burnout. Debunking this erroneous perception, they say: "Our research and consulting work provide clear and consistent evidence that the roots of burnout stretch far beyond the individual into the work environment ... It is not a personality defect or a clinical syndrome. It is an occupational problem." As one of the participants said, "It was great to find out that I wasn't crazy."

160

The amount of time specified by the leaders for recovery and renewal varied from one to four years. Interestingly, 60% classified themselves in the still recovering category. Among the different actions chosen by the participants to further their renewal process are: rest (80%); counselling (73%); sabbaticals and retreats (53%); exercise (53%); vacations (46%); financial adjustments (33%); and identificational repentance (33%).

Although a small percentage indicated always having a Sabbath approach towards rest and renewal, all admitted to the need for more intentionality in both Sabbath rest and the taking of sabbaticals. Many had never taken a sabbatical and were using one of the provided readings, *The Role of Rest and Renewal in Leadership Success*, as a motivator and guide .

Although most of the participants had not taken an official sabbatical as part of their recovery and renewal process, the study revealed that many of them spent significant time in honest reflection about God, themselves and their relationships. Whether they used the standard language of Sabbath/Sabbatical or not, the principles and processes involved in rest and renewal were experienced by many of those in this study.

According to Matthew Henry, God began the Sabbath rest by reflecting on all that He had made. He says: "Having given us the power of reflection, He expects us to use that power, see our way and think of it." In other words, it's about approaching the whole of life from the centrality of his finished work. Herein one can find two of the most significant reminders from the Sabbath day: the centrality of God's perfect provision and the complementarities of life. It combines the unshakable foundation of God's finished work with the blend and balances of various life priorities.

Concluding Thoughts

Embracing the value of the Sabbath or a Sabbatical for the purpose of rest and renewal can never exonerate any organisation from complicity in the burnout of its leaders, or lessen its responsibility to exercise due diligence in looking after the well-being of all. However, in an imperfect world, where even the best of leaders can seriously drop the ball, rediscovering our place in Him who is the final arbiter of our destinies is truly a Psalm 23 encounter. In other words, "He makes me lie down in green pastures; He leads me beside quiet waters. He restores my soul ... Even though I walk through the valley of the shadow of death, I fear no evil, for You are with me" (Psalm 23:2–4).

All the leaders in this study have gone through the valley of death or loss; they have experienced a sense of dying that comes from mismatches within the organisational environment, and have looked into the face of Him who alone is their strength throughout their painful transition. Fortunately, the psalmist doesn't leave us in the valley. As David experienced so powerfully, "You prepare a table before me in the presence of my enemies; You have anointed my head with oil; my cup overflows. Surely goodness and lovingkindness will follow me all the days of my life, and I will dwell in the house of the Lord forever" (Psalm 23:5–6). These leaders, all of them, will never lack a Father who is continually with them, a people who will always love them, Kingdom truth that can forever renew them and a destiny that always awaits them.

They, like many before and after them, will say: "I will lift up my eyes to the mountains; from where does my help come from? My help comes from the Lord" (Psalm 121:1–2). They are among a proven few who will live a better model for the generations to come.

REFERENCES AND CITATIONS

Introduction

Donald Phillips, *Martin Luther King, Jr. On Leadership* (New York, Warner Books, 1998), p.81

Gerhard van Rensburg, *The Leadership Challenge in Africa* (Pretoria, South Africa, Van Schaik, 2007), p.4

Cannistraci, *The Gift of the Apostle* (Ventura CA, Regal Books, 1996), p.50

Donald Miller, *Reinventing American Protestantism*, (Berkeley, CA, University of California

Press, 1997), p.18

Howard Snyder, *The Problem of Wineskins*, (Downers Grove, Ill, Inter-Varsity Press, 1975), p.34

http://www.vineyardbi.org/docs/INTROS/INTRO-Giving_Leadership.pdf

Cannistraci, *The Gift of the Apostle*, p.105 (About the Touchstone)

Chapter One:
Introduction

Cannistraci, *The Gift of the Apostle*, p.81

Richard Daft, *The Leadership Experience* (Mason, Ohio, Thomson: South Western, 2005), p.557

Marcus Buckingham, *The One Thing You Need to Know* (New York, Free Press, 2005), p.59

Ed Vitagliano, *Sandwich or Salvation: Is the Social Gospel Biblical,* American Family Association Journal, October 2009 Issue Taken from the Web on June 10, 2010. http://www.ipcc.cc/SandwichorSalvation.pdf

Albert James Dager, *The World Christian Movement: Evangelism VS Evangelization,* (Media Spotlight, A Biblical Analysis of Religious and Secular Media, Volume 22-Number 1 1999) (Taken from the Web on June 9, 2010)

George Eldon Ladd, *The Gospel of the Kingdom* (Grand Rapids, Michigan, Wm. B. Ferdmans Publishing Co., 1959) Retrieved from the Web on June 9, 2010

Quote by Matthew Henry found in Liberating the Nation on page 12

Dr. Rice Broocks, *Every Nation in our Generation* (Lake Mary Fl, Creation House Press, 2002), p.74

Bob Weiner, *Taking Dominion* (Chosen Books, Old Tappan NJ, 1988) p.158

Stephen McDowell and Mark Beliles, *Liberating the Nations* (Charlottesville, VA, Providence Foundation)

John Pollock, *Wilberforce* (Lion Publishing, Tring, 1977) p. 66

Bruce Winston, *Be a Leader for God's Sake* (Virginia Beach, VA, Regent School of Leadership Studies, 2002),

Dennis Peacocke, *Doing Business God's Way* (Santa Rosa, CA, REBUILD, 1995), p.2

163

Vernon Robbins, *Exploring the Text of Textures* (Harrisburg, PA, Trinity Press, 1996), P.74 (Statement about the reconstruction of the entire social world...)

Dr. Rice Broocks, *Every Nation in our Generation* (Lake Mary Fl, Creation House Press, 2002), p.76 (statement by Herbert Schlossberg)

Stephen McDowell and Mark Beliles, *Liberating the Nations* (Charlottesville, VA, Providence Foundation), p.11 (Statement made by Benjamin Franklin)

Apostles and the Apostolic

Murphy, *Spiritual Gifts and the Great Commission* (Cannistraci page 80 & 93)

Peter Wagner, *Church Quake* p.107-108 (comment about the cessationists)

Cannistraci, *The Gift of the Apostle*, p.28-29 (the use of the term apostle)

Dr. Rice Broocks, *Every Nation in our Generation* (Lake Mary Fl, Creation House Press, 2002), p.178.

Gerhard van Rensburg, *The Leadership Challenge* in Africa (Pretoria, South Africa, Van Schaik, 2007), p.49-50.

Vernon Robbins, *Exploring the Texts of Texture*, p.78

Cannistraci, *The Gift of the Apostle*, p.85

Kevin Conner, *The Church in the New Testament* (Portland, OR, Conner Publications, 1982), p.138

Cannistraci, *The Gift of the Apostle*, p.129

John Eckhardt, *50 Truths Concerning Apostolic Ministry*, (Chicago: Crusaders Ministries, 1994), p.8

Cannistraci, *The Gift of the Apostle*, p.82

Matthew Henry's Unabridged Commentary on the Bible, Christian Classics Ethereal Library http://www.ccel.org/ccel/henry/mhc6.vii.xiii.html Taken from the web on June 19, 2010

Larry Caldwell, *Sent Out: Reclaiming the Spiritual Gift of Apostleship for Missionaries and Churches Today* (Pasadena, CA, William Carey Library, 1992), p.11

Conner, p.151

C. Peter Wagner, *Churches that Pray* (Ventura, CA, Regal Books, 1993), p.139

Cannistraci, p.103

Christina Equippers International, *The Master Builder* (Bible Temple Publishing, 1985), p.147   (Dick Iverson)

Cannistraci, p.57

Article reviewing *The Rise of Christianity* by Rodney Stark; A Book Review by Father John McCloskey, Taken from the Web on June 18, 2010. http://www.catholicity.com/mccloskey/riseofchristianity.html

Donald Guthrie, *The Apostles* (2nd edition) (Grand Rapids Michigan, Zondervan Publishing House, 1992), p.50

Peter Wagner, *The New Apostolic Churches* (Ventura, CA, Regal Books, 1998), p.25

http://www.bjm.org/articles/12/apostolic-teams.html   (Quote from Bill Johnson)

Jonathan David, *Apostolic Strategies Affecting Nations* (Johor Malaysia, 1997), p.511

Cannistraci, *The Gift of the Apostle,* p.103

Guthrie, *The Apostles,* p.84

Ibid, p.86

Dowley, et al, *Eerdmans Handbook to the History of Christianity* (Grand Rapids, Michigan, 1977), p.62   (statement "pattern for the future")

William S. Bernie, *Search for the Early Church* (Wheaton III, Tyndale House, 1978), p.48

Cannistraci, *The Gift of the Apostle*, p.68

Ibid, p.56

Apostolic Leadership Culture

Richard Daft, *The Leadership Experience* (Mason Ohio, Thomson, 2005), p.557.

Kim Cameron and Robert Quinn, Diagnosing and Changing Organizational Culture (San Francisco, Jossy-Bass, 2006), p.16

Erwin McManus, *The Unstoppable Force,* (Loveland, CO, Group Publishing, 2001), p140

Cannistraci, *The Gift of the Apostle,* p.56

Ibid, p.59

Tom Deuschle, *Building People, Building Dreams*, p.102

Cannistraci, *The Gift of the Apostle,* p.65

Howard Snyder, *The Problem of Wineskins* (Downers Grove, III, Inter-Varsity Press, 1976), p.102

James Leo Garret, Jr., *The Concept of the Believers' Church* (Scotts-dale, PA, Herald Press, 1969), p.258

Peter Drucker, *Managing Non-Profit Organizations* (New York, Harper Business, 1990), p.145

Chris Lowney, *Heroic Leadership* (Chicago, IL, Loyola Press, 2003), p.17

Ibid, p.15

James O'Toole, *Leading Change* (New York, Jossey-Bass, 1996), p.9

Chris Lowney, *Heroic Leadership*, p.18

Gerhard van Rensburg, *The Leadership Challenge in Africa* (Pretoria, South Africa, Van Schaik, 2007), p.2

Peter Wagner, *The New Apostolic Churches*, p.212

Cannistraci, *The Gift of the Apostle,* p.173

Belials and McDowell, *Liberating the Nations*, p.3

Amy Lowell

Stephen Mansfield, *Never give In: The Extraordinary character of Winston Churchill*, P.107

Bruce Winston, *Be a Leader for God's Sake*, p.123

Chapter Two
The Drive of Values
Introduction Paragraph

James O'Toole, *Leading Change* (New York, Jossey-Bass, 1996), p.10

Ibid, p.11

Kuczmarski and Kuczmarski, *Values-Based Leadership* (Paramus, NJ, Prentice Hall, 1995)

Dr. Bruce Winston, *Be a Leader for God's Sake* (Virginia Beach, VA, School of Leadership Studies, 2002), p.13

James Kouzes and Barry Posner, *The Leadership Challenge* (San Francisco, Jossey-Bass Publishers, 1995)

Gerhard van Rensburg, *The Leadership Challenge in Africa* (Pretoria, South Africa, Van Schaik, 2007), p.84

Milton Rokeach, *Understanding Human Values* (New York, The Free Press, 1979), p.48

Lyle Schaller, *Getting Things Done*, (Nashville, Abingdon Press, 1986), p.152

Aubrey Malphurs, Values-Driven Leadership (Grand Rapids, Michigan, Baker Books, 2004)

James Kouzes and Barry Posner, *The Leadership Challenge*, p.52

Aubrey Malphurs, *Values-Driven Leadership*, p.20

Desmond Tutu, *No Future without Forgiveness* (London, Random House, 1999)

James Kouzes and Barry Posner, *The Leadership Challenge*, p.29

Danny Silk, *Culture of Honor* (Shippensburg, PA, Destiny Image, 2009), p.61

David Cannistraci, *The Gift of the Apostle* (Ventura CA, Regal Books, 1996), p.90

Kuczmarski and Kuczmarski, *Values-Based Leadership*, p.83

Ibid, p.17

Values the Apostolic and Transformation

Bruce Winston, *Be a Leader for God's Sake*. (Virginia Beach, VA, Regent University, 2002)

Ibid, p.1

Kouzes and Posner, *The Leadership Challenge*, p.115

Senge, Peter, *The Fifth Dimension*, (New York: Doubleday Publishing, 1992) (find the page; 70 not correct)

James O'Toole, *Leading Change* (New York, Jossy-Bass Inc, 1995)

Richard Daft, *The Leadership Challenge* (Mason Ohio, South-Western, 2005) (after: ... "others and service" more than personal gain)

James O'Toole, *Leading Change*, p.11

Gerhard van Rensburg, *The Leadership Challenge in Africa*, p.80

Richard Daft, *The Leadership Challenge* (Mason Ohio, South-Western, 2005), p.153-154

Gary Yukl, *Leadership in Organizations*

Leighton Ford, *Transforming Leadership* (Downers Grove Il, Intervarsity Press,

1991), p.22
Milton Rokeach, *Understanding Human Values*, p.48
Ibid, p.49

Values Discovery and Honor

Geisler and Feinberg, *Introduction to Philosophy*, (Grand Rapids MI, Baker Books 1980) p.367

Martin, Dr Glen, *Biblical Christian Leadership* (Lectures at School of Christian Community Skills, Australia 1992), p.4

Graham Cooke,

McDowell and Beliles, *Liberating the Nations*, (Charlottesville Virginia, Providence Foundation), p.5

Gerhard van Rensburg, *The Leadership Challenge in Africa* (Pretoria, South Africa, Van Schaik, 2007), p.95

Tutu, Desmond, *No Future without Forgiveness*, (London, Random House, 1999), p.10-11

Fawn Parrish, *The Power of Honor* (), p.17

Ibid, p.18

Bruce Winston, *Be a Leader for God's Sake*. (Virginia Beach, VA, Regent University, 2002), p.9

Danny Silk, *Loving on Purpose*

Graham Cooke, *A Divine Confrontation* (Shippensburg, PA, Destiny Image, 1999), p.3

The Value of Knowing and Loving God:

Mike Bickle, *Passion for Jesus* (), p.11

Ibid, p.23

Ibid, p.37

Cannistraci

Ibid, p.36

A.W. Tozer, *The Knowledge of the Holy* (New York, HarperCollins Publishers, 1961), p76

Bill Johnson, *Strengthening Yourself in the Lord* (Shippensburg, PA, Destiny Image, 2007), p.41

Ibid, p.42

Bill Johnson, *The Supernatural Power of a Transformed Mind* (Shippensburg, PA, Destiny Image, 2005), p.44

Burns, James MacGregor, *Leadership* (New York: Harper and Row, 1978), p.437

Chapter Three
Relationally Grounded
Introduction

Article entitled *Chicken Came Before the Egg: "Scientific Proof"* by Tucker Reals on July 14, 2010) (Taken from CBS new.com on July 31, 2010 http://www.

cbsnews.com/stories/2010/07/14/tech/main6676542.shtml)

Erwin McManus, *The Unstoppable Force*, (Loveland, CO, Group Publishing, 2001), p.166

Graham Cooke, *A Divine Confrontation* (Shippensburg, PA, Destiny Image, 1999), p.68

Christian Equippers International, *The Master Builder* (1985), p.147

Margaret Wheatley, *Leadership and the New Science: Learning about Science from an Orderly Universe* (San Francisco, Berrett-Koehler, 1999), p11

Gerhard van Rensburg, *The Leadership Challenge in Africa*, p.49 (put after "... focus for growth and productivity."

Chris Lowney, *Heroic Leadership* (Chicago, IL, Loyola Press, 2003), p.170

Ibid, p.176

Mark Conner, *Transforming Your Church* (Kent, England, Sovereign Press, 2000), p.70

Richard Daft, *The Leadership Experience*, p.199

The New Mystics, John Crowder (Destiny Image, Shippensburg PA, 2006) p.187

Madan Birla and Cecilia Miller Marshal, Balanced *Life and Leadership Excellence* (Memphis TN, The Balance Group, 1997), p.76-77 (Taken from Daft, p.203)

Family and Fathering

Shapiro, J. Schrof, J. Tharp, M. & Friedman, D. (1995) *Honor thy children.* US News and World Report, p.39   (put after ....target of child abuse)

David Popenoe, *Life without Father.* (Boston, Harvard University Press, 1999)

Bill Muhlenberg, *The Facts of Fatherlessness* Retrieved on March 17, 2010 http://jmm.aaa.net.au/articles/5399.htm

Heidi Holland, *Fatherlessness*, Retrieved on March 17, 2010 http://www.dinnerwithmugabe.com/Columns/Fartherlessness.html

Frank Damazio, *The Vanguard Leader*, (Portland, Bible Temple, 1994), p.17

Richard Daft, *The Leadership Experience*, p.256

Cannistraci, *The Gift of the Apostle*, p.117

Taken from the Barna Group Website, Article entitled: *Twentysomethings Struggle to Find Their Place in Christian Churches*, September 24, 2003. Retrieved from the internet at www.barna.org/barna-update/artical/5-barna-update/127

Randall Kittle, *Is There a Father in the House*, Retrieved on March 20, 2010, http://www.livingwaterpublications.org/fathers.html

Ibid

Alfred Eldersheim, *Sketches of Jewish Social Life*, Chapter 8, (Taken from On-line Books Feb 4, 2010 at http://www.ccel.org/ccel/edersheim/sketches.html)

Ibid

David Williams, *Paul's Metaphors: Their Contest and Character* Peabody, MA, Hendrickson Publications, 1999)

Rice Broocks, *Every Nation in our Generation* (Lake Mary, FL: Creation House Press, 2002), p.146&149   Cannistraci, The Gift of the Apostle, p.116

Winston, *Be A Leader for God's Sake*, p.29

Richard Daft, *The Leadership Challenge*, p.199-202

Apostolic Teams (2009), Retrieved on November 8, 2009 from http://www.bjm.org/articles/12/apostolic-teams.html

Chaim Waxman, The Jewish Father: Past and Present, Retrieved on Feb 6, 2010 at https://www.policyarchive.org/bitstream/handle/10207/10197/TheJewishFatherPastAndPresent.pdf

Ibid

William M. Ramsay, Historical Commentary of the Pastoral Epistles, (Grand Rapids, Michigan, Kregel Publications, 1996) p.66

Vernon Robbins, Exploring the Texture of Texts, p.83

Cannistraci, The Gift of the Apostle, p.117

Ibid, p.128

The Power of Multigenerational Living

Ben Witherington III, *The Acts of the Apostles: A Socio-Rhetorical Commentary*, p.474

Rela M. Griffin, *Celebration and Renewal: Rites of Passage in Judaism* (Jewish Publication Society, 1993) http://www.myjewishlearning.com/life/Life_Events/Lifecycle_Ritual/Why_Lifecycle_Rituals/Lifecycle_and_Tradition.shtml

Mark Conner, *Transforming Your Church*, (Kent, England, Sovereign World, 2000) p.150

Ibid p.148

Sharon Graham and John Graham, *Together Again: A creative guide to multigenerational living*. Retrieved from the internet on August 6, 2010 http://www.togetheragainbook.com/

Mark Conner, *Transforming Your Church*, p.148

Webster 1828 Dictionary of the English Language, Facsimile Edition

The Secrets to Aging Well, WebMD; Nov 29, 2011

Albert Laszio Barabasi, *Linked* (London, Penguin Books, 2003), p.3

Asmal, et.al, *Mandela in His own Words* (New York, Little, Brown and Company, 2003), p.236

Ibid, p.272

Conclusion

Larry Crabb, *Connecting* (Nashville, Word Publishing, 1997), p.191

The New Mystics, John Crowder (Destiny Image, Shippensburg PA, 2006) p.123-124

Chapter Four
Mission-directed Team Leadership
Introduction

John Maxwell, 21 *Irrefutable Laws of Leadership*, (Nashville TN, Thomas Nelson, 2001)

John Maxwell, *The Miracle of Teamwork*; Retrieved from Web on August 17, 2010 from http://www.successmagazine.com/Article-Headline/PARAMS/article/277/channel/19

Danny Silk, *Culture of Honor*, p.60, 2nd Paragraph

Jon Katzenbach and Douglas Smith, *The Wisdom of Teams* (New York: Harvard Business School Press, 1993)   (Put after mutual accountability)

Richard Daft, *The Leadership Experience*

Katzenbach and Smith, *The Wisdom of Teams*

Nelson Mandela, *In His Own Words*, p.101

Ibid, p.109

Nehemiah's Mission-directed Leadership Team
1st Paragraph

Nelson Mandela, *In His Own Words*, p.165

McClung, Floyd, *You See Bones/I See an Army*, (Cape Town, Struik Christian Books, 2008)

Ibid

- Common Purpose

Richard Daft, *The Leadership Experience*, p.398

Ibid

Donald Phillips, *Martin Luther King, Jr. on Leadership*, p.162

Ibid, p.164

- Good Communication

Richard Daft, *The Leadership Experience*, p.343

Ibid, p.342

Katzenbach and Smith, *The Wisdom of Teams*, p.48

- A Continuous Supply...

John Maxwell, The 17 *Indisputable Laws of Teamwork*, p.34

Ray Stedman, *The Walls of Jerusalem Rebuilt*

Katzenbach and Smith, *The Wisdom of Teams*, p.45-46

Danny Silk, *The Culture of Honor*, p.75

Blanchard, Randolph and Grazier, *Go Team*, p.47

- Currency of Trust

Paul Lencioni, *The Five Dysfunctions of a Team*, p.195

Richard Daft, *The Leadership Experience*, p.409

- Well Planned Strategy

Ibid, p.510

Nelson Mandela: *In His Own Words*, p.164

Gerhard van Rensburg, *The Leadership Challenge in Africa*, p.86-87

- Flexibility and Adaptability

Bob Briner and Ray Pritchard, *The Leadership Lessons of Jesus*, p.115

Richard Daft, *The Leadership Experience*, p.634

Katzenbach and Smith, *The Wisdom of Teams*, p.150

- In summary

John Maxwell, The 17 *Indisputable Laws of Teamwork*, p.3 (Put after Einstein's remark)

Fritsch, in *The Layman's Bible Commentary* has referred to Genesis as "the starting point of all theology (Quoted from The Zondervan Encyclopedia of the Bible, p.679)

Bob Deffenbaugh, *A Walk through the Book of Genesis*

Genesis Model for Team

Daft, *The leadership Experience*, p.594

- Team God

Cannistraci, *Gift of the Apostle*, p.69-74

Webster's 1828, Facsimile Edition

Daft, *The Leadership Experience*, p.343

Parkinson, C. *Crucial Conversation*, (New York: McGraw Hill, 2002) p.1

Gerhard van Rensburg, *The Leadership Challenge in Africa*, p.76

Daft, *The leadership Experience*, p.438

- Team man

Laurie Beth Jones, *Teaching your Team to Fish*, p.72

Daft, p.63

Ibid, p. 437

Ibid, p.454

Ibid, p.194

Chris Lowey, Heroic Leadership, (Chicago, Loyola Press, 2003), p.28

Daft, p.129

Jim Collins, Good to Great, p.63

Dr Larry Crabb, Connecting, p.9

- Team man and God

Ibid, p.15

Nelson Mandela, In His Own Words, p.146

Andy Stanley, Focus on Strategic Leadership, p.75

Rainer and Geiger, Simple Church, p.197

Hackman and Johnson, Leadership: A Communications Perspective, p.191

The Art of Powerful Questions: Catalyzing insight, innovation and Action by Vogt, Brown and Isaacs, 2003 p.2

Ibid, p.1

Conclusion

Hackman and Johnson, p.202

John Maxwell, The 17 Indisputable Laws of Teamwork, p.13

Chapter Five
Global and Innovative
Introduction

Ed Silvoso, *Transformation: Change the Market Place and you Change the World* (Ventura, CA, Regal Books, 2007), p.42-43

Kevin Conner, *Church of the New Testament*

Cannistraci, *Gift of the Apostle,* p.180

From Paul to the...

Robbins, *The Texture of Texts*, p.86-87

Jonathan David, *Apostolic Strategies Affecting Nation*, (Malaysia, David Publishing, 1997), p. 479

Chris Lowney, *Heroic Leadership*, p.28

Ibid, p.7

Ibid

Howard Snyder, *The Problem of Wineskins* (Put after, to faith and relationships)

Hammond, P (2009) *How the reformation changed the world,* Retrieved November 9, 2009 from http://www.frontline.org.za/articles/howreformation_changedworld.htm

Wagner, *Churchquake,* p.57

Ibid

Wagner, *The New Apostolic Churches.* Ventura, p.18

Ibid, p.17

Global Competence in Africa

http://www.wholesomewords.org/missions/bliving6.html

Missionary Biographies David Livingstone, by Florence Huntington Jensen

http://www.irisministries.com/about-our-mission.cfm

Lundy & Visser, *South Africa: Reasons to Believe,* (Cape Town, Aardvark Press, 2003), p.101

Lovemore Mbigi, *The Spirit African Leadership,* (Rensburg, Knowres Publishing, 2005), p.5

Ibid

B.J. van der Walt, *When African and Western Cultures Meet,* (Potchefstroom, ICCA, 2006), p.192

Lovemore Mbigi, *The Spirit of African Leadership,* p.69

Gerhard van Rensburg, *The Leadership Challenge in Africa,* p.49

Black, Morrison & Gregersen, *Global Explorers,* (New York, Routledge, 1999), p.112

Ibid

Wikipedia, Kofi Annan (http://www.betterworldheroes.com/pages-a/annan-quotes.htm)

Desmond Tutu, *No Future Without Forgiveness,* (London, Random House, 1999), p.35

Nelson Mandela, *In His Own Words*, (New York, Time Warner, 2003), p.502

McCall and Hollenbeck, *Developing Global Executives,* (Boston, HBSP, 2002), p.22

Robert Greenleaf, *Servant Leadership,* (Ramsey, NJ, Paulist Press, 1977), p.28

McCall and Hollenbeck, *Developing Global Executives* p.103

Lovemore Mbigi, *The Spirit of African Leadership*, p.76

McCall and Hollenbeck, *Developing Global Executives* p.104

B.J. van der Walt, *Understanding and Rebuilding Africa*, p.140

Mobley & McCall Jr., *Advances in Global Leadership*, (New York, Elsevier, 2001), p.41

Ibid p.5

McCall and Hollenbeck, *Developing Global Executives* p.108

Lovemore Mbigi, *The Spirit of African Leadership* (Kenneth Kuanda's quote)

McCall and Hollenbeck, *Developing Global Executives* p.109

A Pauline Model for Global Competence

Ben Witherington, *Paul's Letter to the Romans*, (Grand Rapids, MI, Ferdmans Publishing Co., 2004), p.2

Ibid p.34

Ibid p.10

Robert Greenleaf, *Servant Leadership* (Ramsey, NJ. Paulist Press, 1977), p.49

Ibid p.227

Gerhard van Rensburg, *The Leadership Challenge in Africa,* (Pretoria, South Africa, Van Schaik Publishers, 2007), p.57

Ibid (Servants within the community)

International Journal of Leadership Studies, Vol. 3 Issue 2, 2008, pp. 212-222 ©2008 School of Global Leadership & Entrepreneurship, Regent University ISSN 1554-3145, www.regent.edu/ijls   (The Globe study)

Ibid   (globe study)

Broocks, *Every Nation in our Generation*, p.186

Donald Guthrie, *The Apostles* (Grand Rapids MI, Zondervan Publishing, 1975), p.139

Cannistraci, *The Gift of the Apostle*, p.177

Witherington, *Paul's Letter to the Romans*, p.9

Ibid

Neil Cole, *The Organic Church*, p.124

C. Peter Wagner, *Church Quake* (Ventura, CA, Regal Books, 1999), p.15   (Grass root churches)

Neil Cole, *The Organic Church*, p.24

Cannistraci, *The Gift of the Apostle*, p.179

Robert W. Keidel, *Seeing Organizational Patterns* (Washington DC: Beard Books, 1995), p.100

Robert W. Keidel, *Seeing Organizational Patterns*, p.6

Ibid

173

Ibid, p.9

Nelson Mandela, *In His Own Words*, p.157

Robert W. Keidel, *Seeing Organizational Patterns*, p.24

Ibid, p.27

Evidence of this pattern exists in Acts 13:42-47; 14:1-6; 17:1-5; 18:4; 19:8-9.

Robert W. Keidel, *Seeing Organizational Patterns*, p.29   (Put after, horizontal decision making.)

Augustine Shutte, *Ubuntu; an ethic for a new South Africa* (Pietermaritzburg, SA Cluster Publications, 2001)

Gerhard Van Rensburg, *The Leadership Challenge in Africa* (Pretoria, SA, Van Schailk Publishers, 2007)

The Apostolic: New Alliances and Networks

Barabasi, *Linked*, p.6

Ibid, p.7

Cannistraci, *The Gift of the Apostle*, p.185

Conner, *The New Testament Church*, p.151

Wagner, *Churchquake*, p.126

Cannistraci, *The Gift of the Apostle*, p.192

Ibid, p.196

Conclusion

Cannistraci, *The Gift of the Apostle*, p.64-65

Robbins, *The Text of Textures*, p.125

Gryskiewics, Stanley S., *Positive Turbulence* (San Francisco, Jossey-Bass, 1999), p. 8

Chapter Six
Spirit-filled Enablement and the Long Haul
Introduction

Dr. Richard J. Krejcir, *What is going on with the Pastors in America?* Retrieved from http://www.intothyword.org/articles_view.asp?articleid=36562&colum nid=3958

Ibid

Bill Johnson, *When Heaven Invades Earth* (Shippensburg, PA, Destiny Image Publishers, 2003), p.74

R. A, Torrey, *The Person and Work of the Hole Spirit* (New Kensington, PA, Whitaker House, 1996), p.82

Michael Brown, *Whatever Happened to the Power of God* (Shippensburg, PA, Destiny Image Publications, 1991), p.25

The Apostolic and the Holy Spirit

Cannistraci, *The Gift of the Apostle*, p.68
Ibid
Cannistraci, *The Gift of the Apostle,* p.76

Paul Yonggi Cho, *The Holy Spirit my Senior Partner* (Altamonte Springs, Fl, Creation House, 1989), p.20
Cannistraci, *The Gift of the Apostle,* p.68
Paul Yonggi Cho, *The Holy Spirit My Senior Partner*, p.28
Ibid, p.89

Marion Murillo, *Fresh Fire* (San Ramon, Anthony Douglas Publishing), p.114
Bill Johnson, *When Heaven Invades Earth*, p.87

E. M. Bounds, *E. M. Bounds on Prayer* (New Kensington, PA, Whitaker House, 1997), p.69
(Brother Lawrence quote)
Ibid, p.13
Bill Johnson, *When Heaven Invades Earth*, p.64
Ibid, p.92
E. M. Bounds, *E. M. Bounds on Prayer,* p.182

Bill Johnson, *The Supernatural Power of a Transformed Mind* (Shippensburg, PA, Destiny Image Publishers, 2005), p.49

Supernatural Living

Cannistraci, *The Gift of the Apostle*, p.159
Bill Johnson, *When Heaven Invades Earth*, p.141

Bill Johnson, *When Heaven Invades Earth*, p.94
Sanders, Oswald, *Spiritual Leadership*, (Chicago, Moody Press, 1976), p.33

Dallas Willard, *Renovation of the Heart* (Colorado Springs, CO, NavPress, 2002), p.3
Bill Johnson, *Release the power of Jesus* (Shippensburg, CA, Destiny Image Publishers, 2009), p.164

Rest and Renewal
Gerhard Van Rensburg, *The Leadership Challenge in Africa* (p.43)
Ray Steadman, *The Seventh Day: Jesus is our Sabbath Rest*   http://ldolphin.org/sabbathrest.html
Matthew Henry's Commentary of the Bible, Taken from the Web on Feb 20, 2010 http://www.searchgodsword.org/com/mhc-com/view.cgi?book=ge
-http://www.mindtools.com/pages/article/newHTE_93.htm

Christina Maslach and Michael Leiter, *The Truth about Burnout*, (San Francisco, Jossey-Bass, 1997) p.42& 148

Os Guinness & John Seel, *No God But God* (Chicago, IL, Moody Press, 1992), 33

Vernon Robbins, *Exploring the Texture of Texts*, (Harrisburg, Trinity Press, 1996) p.41

Sarah Ledoux, *The Effects of Sleep Deprivation on the Brain and Behavior* (Biology 202 Web paper) http://serendip.brynmawr.edu/exchange/node/1690

Jordon S. Rubin, *The Makers Diet* (Lake Mary FL, Siloam Publishers, 2004)

-Elmer A. Josephson, *God's Keys to Health and Happiness* (Old Tappan NJ: Fleming H. Revell Company, 1976), p. 163

-John O'Neil, *The Paradox of Success* (New York, Penguin, 2004)

-James Strong, *The New Strong's Exhaustive Concordance of the Bible* (Nashville TN, Thomas Nelson Publishers, 1990)

-Laurie Beth Jones, *Jesus, CEO* (New York, Hyperion, 1995)

-James Ryle, *How to Win without being Wicked* (Franklin TN, Grace Center, 2010)

Chapter 7
Conclusion

Howard Snyder, *The Problem with Wineskins: Church Structure in a Technological Age* (Downers Grove, Ill, Inter-varsity Press, 1976), p.16

Ibid, p.154

Ibid, p.157

George Eldon Ladd, *The Gospel of the Kingdom* (Grand Rapids, Michigan, Wm. Ferdmans Publishing Co., 1959)

David Cannistraci, *The Gift of the Apostle*, p.65

James O'Toole, *Leading Change*, p.11

Fawn Parrish, *The Power of Honor*, p.18

A.W. Tozer, *The Knowledge of the Holy*, p.76

Erwin McManus, *The Unstoppable Force*, p.166

Bill Johnson, *Apostolic Teams* (2009), Retrieved on November 8, 2009 from http://www.bjm.org/articles/12/apostolic-teams.html

Erwin McManus, *The Unstoppable Force*, p.1

Ibid, p.110

McCall and Hollenbeck, *Developing Global Executives*, p.22

Cannistraci, *The Gift of the Apostle*, p.185

ABOUT THE AUTHOR

Bill experienced a radical conversion to Christ while attending the University of Tennessee on a wrestling scholarship in 1979. Along with his wife Connie, he began fulltime Christian ministry in 1981. Up until 1986, Bill and Connie pioneered and led campus churches in California, Arizona and New Mexico. Besides ministering on university campuses throughout the Western United States, Bill began traveling into various African countries in 1982. Then in 1987 Bill and Connie moved to Johannesburg, South Africa. They pioneered the His People Christian Church which grew to a couple thousand, and became an apostolic base for church planting in Africa. Over the next 18 years Bill worked with leaders and teams to plant churches and campus ministries in every major city in South Africa. He also served leaders and churches in Namibia, Zimbabwe, Zambia, the Democratic Republic of the Congo, Botswana, Tanzania, Kenya, Uganda, Nigeria, Ghana, Sierra Leone and the Ivory Coast.

In 2005 Bill and Connie established a second base in Nashville, Tennessee, while simultaneously moving their African base to Cape Town, South Africa. Over the next 5 years they served multiple churches and leaders in Africa and the United States; their focuses being revival, reformation and cultural transformation. From 2007-2009 they led the leadership team for the 7000 member His People Church in Cape Town, South Africa.

Bill and Connie are currently pioneering a leadership alliance called BMosaic. BMosaic is a gathering of Jesus-centered, relationally-connected and kingdom-minded leaders who are partnering together for the purpose of bringing the glory of His kingdom everywhere. They are also currently launching a new church in Cape Town called Journey of Grace.

Bill holds a Masters degree in organizational leadership and a Doctorate in strategic leadership. His wife, Connie is the founder and director of Redemptive Solutions, a Christian counseling practice. Bill's apostolic ministry and Connie's prophetic ministry are teaming together with a diversity of leaders throughout the body of Christ to release heaven on earth. They have three sons, Ben, Adam, and Ethan, and one daughter, Melody.

Printed in Great Britain
by Amazon.co.uk, Ltd.,
Marston Gate.